JOHN SALVESON

THE PSYCHOLOGICAL REPORT

THE
PSYCHOLOGICAL REPORT
Use and Communication of Psychological Findings

WALTER G. KLOPFER, Ph.D.
Associate Professor of Psychology
Director of Clinical Training,
University of Portland

With a Foreword by
Leopold Bellak, M. D.

GRUNE & STRATTON   New York   London

Figures 2 and 3 were reprinted with the permission of
The Psychological Corporation, New York, New York.

Fourth Printing   November, 1972

Grune & Stratton, Inc.
111 Fifth Avenue
New York, New York 10003

Library of Congress Catalog Card Number 60-7176
International Standard Book Number 0-8089-0236-9

Printed in the United States of America

CONTENTS

FOREWORD

THE PSYCHOLOGICAL REPORT constitutes a distilla-
tion of all we can learn about a person by using our psychological tools, as predicated upon our theories and working
hypotheses. The Report is a primary document of psychology
as a science, of our methods of study and is a personal document
(in the sense in which Allport has used the term*) of the psychologist who wrote the report.

If one were to study the development of clinical psychology
in the recent past, one could do worse than to investigate a cross
section of reports written, say, over the last ten years. Such research, I believe, would show a progression from the rather
naive, shotgun type of ill-assorted tests based upon the "sign"
approach that prevailed in the immediate postwar years to
the slow emergence of ego psychological thinking, an awareness of limitations of our instruments, and a sophistication
concerning the different levels of inference in the clinical interview and the test material.

The Test Report also reveals something of the changing
nature of the communication between the allied disciplines of
psychology, psychiatry, anthropology, and social work: if
psychologists have had to sharpen their tools, psychiatrists
have had to learn that the "psychological" does not constitute
a slot machine which delivers a diagnosis upon insertion of a
request slip for testing—as it sometimes seemed in the late
1940's. In the first place, the psychiatrist is likely to receive
information in proportion to the trouble he takes in stating
his request specifically; and in the second place, he has to be
able to evaluate the test findings within the total set of data.

In the Test Report, then, the study of man meets a crucial
challenge. The wonder of it is that the present volume is the

* Allport, G. W., The use of personal documents in psychological science. Social
Science Research Council, New York, 1942.

first one to my knowledge dedicated in its entirety to this topic!

The fact is that report writing has been done rather haphazardly most of the time, when training courses, intensive inquiries, and the establishment of definite frames of reference need to be the order of the day.

A symposium sponsored jointly by the Society for Projective Techniques and the American Psychiatric Association* was one of the steps in the direction of improving test reporting. Dr. Klopfer, who also participated in that symposium, presents another significant step towards that goal in the present volume.

In his own crisp style, Dr. Klopfer reviews the various general problems of report writing illuminatingly and in detail. He proposes his own closely reasoned form for organizing a psychological report.

Dr. Leonard Small and myself encouraged Dr. Klopfer to undertake this venture; in reading his manuscript, we had occasion to discuss some differences of opinion. For instance, my personal preference is for a more detailed consideration of adaptive and defensive functioning than Dr. Klopfer provides; possibly, also, I have a liking for an even closer progression from primary concrete test data to abstract formulation than discussed in the present volume. However, I would not be surprised if Dr. Klopfer's approach will be the one to have the widest possible appeal, especially by virtue of a variety of excellent features. Among these, I want to emphasize particularly his attention to a comparison and systematic evaluation of variations in responses to stimuli in different tests, as when he compares the "rows" in his outline. His insistence on the recording of discrepant features will, among other things, be a goldmine for heuristic hunches and research. His case discussions should prove excellent classroom material.

In short, I believe that Dr. Walter Klopfer has contributed a monograph which I feel certain will become a standard source in the teaching and practice of clinical psychology.

LEOPOLD BELLAK, M.D.

* Bellak, L., Chairman, Symposium: Psychological Test Reporting: A Problem in Communication Between Psychologists and Psychiatrists. The Journal of Nervous and Mental Disease, Volume 129, No. 1, July, 1959.

INTRODUCTION

THIS VOLUME is based upon the belief that the findings of psychological assessment procedures are meaningful, basically consistent and communicable to others. It is assumed that the hypotheses culled from tests, however speculative, can be evaluated in terms of logical and empirical demonstrability.

The viewpoints herein expressed are the result of contact with many friends and colleagues over the years. All of them have my deep appreciation even though they are too numerous to cite by name. I am especially grateful to Leopold Bellak and my colleague of many years, Gordon Filmer-Bennett. Both of these have read the entire manuscript in detail and made many valuable suggestions. I also wish to express my appreciation to Earl S. Taulbee, who not only cooperated with Gertrude J. Williams and myself in the preparation of Chapter 9, but contributed heavily to the organizational scheme described in Chapter 5.

Finally, I wish to express my gratitude to my father, Bruno Klopfer, who introduced me to the field of clinical psychology at a tender age and provided me with guidance throughout the ensuing years.

WALTER G. KLOPFER
Portland, Oregon

January, 1960

1
PURPOSE

THE ESSENTIAL purposes of psychological reports primarily concern three different individuals: the referent who has requested the evaluation, the clinician who is providing the evaluation, and the client whose whole future may be at issue. Each will be taken up separately, after which some general comments will be made.

Concerns of the Referent

The referent, whoever he may be, is generally concerned with a number of practical issues involving the client under consideration, such as employment, disposition, the prediction of antisocial behavior, and so forth. He would like this information in the form of a record which will be maximally useful in considering all further issues concerning the client.

Hammond and Allen (12) feel that a report must be functional to serve this purpose. They describe the usual "psychometric" report as being stereotyped and deride its "quantitative" nature as contributing heavily to a stereotype which detracts from its utility. In their view, the report must be adapted mainly to the so-called primary reader. To this end they suggest that the primary reader be thoroughly studied and that plans be made to meet his needs and insure his understanding. They suggest that, whenever possible, specific behavior be referred to and predicted. Both immediate and long range recommendations might be included in the report, as long as the clinician is keenly aware of the limits within which the reader can act on these recommendations, as well as the limits of his capacity to understand the material described. Accordingly, different kinds of reports might be best for psychologists, those in related professions, and those in relatively unrelated professions.

The implication is that as the reader's education and training decreases, the report must become progressively simpler. However, it is my feeling that another viewpoint might also be applicable: Many of the concepts utilized routinely by clinical psychologists are only seemingly complex and could just as well be translated into common, predictive language easily communicated to anyone. For example, the matter of "oedipal involvement" might be referred to in a report as follows: "The patient has always had a very close relationship with his mother. Her own feelings toward him being mixed, she has alternately bound him to her with an excessive display of affection and made him insecure within the relationship by rejection and coyness. The fact that the patient has not been able to resolve this relationship has made it very difficult for him to look upon other women objectively and to relate to them in a mature and rational manner. Also, his great involvement with his mother, who has often used him as a medium through which to express mixed feelings toward the father, has distorted his relationship with men so that they are often seen as rivals rather than allies." Virtually every complex statement can be translated into such generally comprehensible terminology.

Holzberg, Alessi, and Wexler (13) agree with many others that the psychological report should meet the specific needs of the referent in a specific situation. The report should be detailed and pertinent to the question at hand here and now. It should also include test evidence (a matter which will be taken up in greater detail in a later chapter). They aptly suggest that the clinician should not restrict his communicative efforts to the formal report but should freely participate in the discussion following, irrespective of the limitations and uses of the psychological findings. This point seems worthy of considerable attention. Too many times the referent finds himself frustrated by the fact that psychological reports in written form constitute the sole bridge between himself and the psychologist. Oral communication has many advantages as a supplement. The referent can ask questions concerning areas which have not been sufficiently clarified, he can question the psychologist as to apparent discrepancies and discover the basic unifying variables in the personality of the patient as revealed by the various assessment procedures, including his own approach. In addition, the personal and professional relationship between the referent and the clinical psychologist will certainly be improved by frequent contact.

Certain kinds of referents present unique problems in defining the purpose of the psychological report. Psychiatrists probably most frequently refer cases to the clinical psychologist; that certain professional and other problems occasionally arise between psychiatrists and psychologists hardly requires detailed consideration. Some psychiatrists would like to limit the psychologist's role to assessment and tend to resent his offering specific classificatory suggestions which seemingly usurp the diagnostic role. Some are quite reasonably irritated by the psychologist's assumption of omnipotence as implied by the way in which he couches his report. What the psychiatrist wants is help in his task of evaluation and treatment planning and he usually has respect and consideration for the clinical psychologist with whom he is associated. He is not apt to be enchanted by esoteric language or by attempts on the part of the psychologist to impress him with his superior knowledge and sophistication. On the other hand, psychiatrists may employ psychological consultants with inadequate training who are not capable of representing psychological knowledge at its best.

Where the referent is a physician who is not practicing psychiatry and regards his own psychological sophistication more highly than is justified, he may be particularly disturbed by the psychologist's tacit assumption to the contrary. If, on the other hand, he relies excessively upon the psychological report for making his medical decisions he may endow the psychologist with more responsibility than is reasonable or justified. It is especially important in this case to communicate psychological findings in comprehensible ways that will enable him to make the kind of decisions necessary. The psychologist, in his attempts to impress, may give a psychological report to the general practitioner which has little relationship to the problems which initiated the referral.

As the profession of the referent becomes increasingly distant in terms of common interest and common language, it becomes increasingly necessary for the clinical psychologist to make the psychological report appropriate and to the point. Not only must the primary reader be considered, but also those who may utilize the report for other purposes. Hammond and Allen (12) seem to feel that the report should include raw behavioral data if it is to be used for research purposes; however, the desirability of such a practice is questionable, since most researchers probably prefer to go back to the tests themselves rather than rely upon reports with all their manifold purposes.

From the viewpoint of the psychiatric social worker the report should again be specifically designed to aid in the decisions at hand. The question may be whether a patient should be considered for discharge or rehabilitation, or whether adjustment in an adult nursing home is likely or unlikely. How adequately the report meets these needs depends on the degree to which they are specifically taken up. The report which delves deeply into the dynamics and genetics of the personality may be an enjoyable intellectual exercise, but of very little practical value. If the social worker is not trained in the psychiatric area, the increased differences in terminology must be taken into account.

Teachers also make use of psychological reports. Here a compromise must be made between the psychologist's desire to impress upon the teacher the limitations of his predictive instruments and the teacher's need to have specific information bearing upon her administrative decisions (e.g., an I Q). Here again, oral discussions rather than written correspondence would probably greatly facilitate communication. Psychological reports oriented toward industrial consultant work and the individual therapist must again take into account the referent's needs, but not to the exclusion of those of the client or the other parties involved.

Concerns of the Clinician

The clinician is usually sufficiently mature so that he can face the over-determined nature of his motivation in writing the psychological report. Certainly he is motivated in large part by his desire to help the referent and the client by communicating his findings and by making clear the nature of the problems and how they can best be solved. At the same time, he is likely to be motivated by his desire for status and prestige and by wishes to impress the reader with his skill and acumen.

He may also occasionally be motivated by hostile and aggressive impluses toward one or the other of the persons involved and so use the report as a vehicle for making deleterious remarks. He may become involved with the patient to the point of inadvertently playing down some aspects and exaggerating others, he may seek to demonstrate the predictive efficiency of one psychological instrument at the expense of another, or he may go off into literary flights to demonstrate his verbal skill to a potentially vast audience of colleagues, students, or staff members in an agency. It is unlikely that all these needs could be met along with the primary purpose of the psychological report, communication. These additional needs are distorting factors and interfere with the communicative process. They are professionally undesirable and should be dealt with accordingly.

Concerns of the Client

If the client were asked the purpose of the psychological report, his answer might vary with his condition of the moment. If he is keenly aware of his emotional illness and greatly desires help, he may regard the report as a means of being better understood and more appropriately treated by a potential therapist. On the other hand, he may consider the psychological procedure to be highly superfluous and resent the time taken for this seemingly tangential matter. He may regard the psychological examination as an invasion of his privacy and consider the psychological report an insidious document designed to blacken his name and besmirch his character. (Needless to say, no ethical clinical psychologist will ever give copies of his report to the patient or otherwise communicate to him its exact contents. The matter of the interpretation of psychological findings to the patient is an integral part of counseling or therapy and should be dealt with in that context.)

In all fairness to the client, we should remember that the psychological report is mainly for his benefit and that whatever problems either the referent or the clinician may have should not be allowed to emerge to the detriment of the client whose emotional adjustment is at stake. His personality picture should remain relatively untouched and unscathed by the personal problems of the professional people charged with his evaluation and care. For this reason it is always best that the psychological report, before being presented in its final form, be evaluated by at least two people so as to lessen as much as possible the effects of personal bias, prejudice, or projection.

Summary

The purpose of the psychological report has been discussed from the viewpoint of the various participants involved. Leaving aside distorting motives, it appears that the referent requires information which will help him in practical ways and which the clinician should be equipped to give him. The client has as his main interest the understanding and effective treatment of his difficulties by the agency personnel charged with this part of the job. The more that the client's role in this situation can be kept in mind, the less will either the clinician or the referent be inclined to look upon the test as an intellectual exercise or battle of wits. If the purpose of helping the client cannot be served by the psychological report, its basic utility is doubtful.

2

FOCUS

THE MOST GENERAL problem encountered by people attempting to use psychological reports for practical purposes is lack of focus. Inexperienced and poorly trained psychologists have a tendency to put together an indigestible mass of discreet observations and a "cook book" list of signs and indicators without any sort of overview or attempt to apply these to the problems which prompted the original referral. In the study by Garfield, Heine, and Leventhal (10), the psychological reports that had been rated were criticized for lack of clarity and focus, as well as for poor organization and the lack of behavioral referents. The authors infer that the use of test data in psychological reports may therefore be a rather dubious matter at best.

In a study by Ullmann, Berkman, and Hamister (27) an attempt was made to relate psychological reports to behavior and probable benefit from placement in a nursing home. The two measures used to predict subsequent adjustment in a nursing home were the psychological reports themselves and the length of the hospitalization. Interestingly enough, it was discovered that psychological reports, when added to data concerning length of hospitalization, did not materially increase the accuracy of prediction for adjustment in the nursing home. However, it was further found that reports specifically dealing with conformity in a group situation predicted nursing-home adjustment beyond chance, whereas the routine type of report did not. The interjudge reliability in making predictions of this kind from psychological reports was only fair, but would probably have been aided by increased specificity. This study seems clearly to indicate a need for greater focusing of the report. Foci which can be employed are reviewed below.

Diagnosis

There are many settings in which diagnosis of some sort is a crucial matter and others in which it is not. In most medical settings, such as neuropsychiatric hospitals, the neuropsychiatric sections of general hospitals, and mental hygiene clinics organized with the usual professional team, it is usually necessary to classify the patient in some way and this classification is usually partly based on the results of the psychological examination. However, a focus on nosological classification may well distort the psychologist's thinking and verbalizations. He may become so concerned with pathology and abnormality that he completely fails to recognize the individual's assets and strengths. A preoccupation with the identification of pathology may lead to an excessive use of the so-called diagnostic signs. Most of these signs were arrived at by comparing patients diagnosed as possessing a certain psychiatric condition with a "normal control group." The use of such group comparisons for individual prediction is a most hazardous procedure, especially when no cross-validation study has been carried out, as is unfortunately often the case. Also, many of these signs are nondiscriminatory, readily identifying a great many different psychiatric conditions without clearly distinguishing among them. Psychological tests might better be used for diagnostic purposes by focusing upon phenomena found at the level of private communication which could then be integrated with the material at the levels of conscious and public communication* collected by the psychiatrist and the social worker as part of a comprehensive evaluation of the individual.

Of course, diagnosis cannot be thought of as referring exclusively to nosological classification. There are many situations in which the diagnosis itself is not at issue, such as in clearly defined psychosomatic conditions. In this case diagnosis may refer to personological classification, making it slightly more difficult, though not impossible, for the psychologist to resort to stereotypy. Accordingly, psychological tests may be used to elicit "signs of aggression" or "signs of homosexuality" in much the same way as schizophrenic signs. The absurdity of this

---

* For a description of private and public communication see Chapter 8.

procedure was clearly demonstrated in some of the recent work of Hooker (14). Using homosexuality as an example, she demonstrated very clearly that the signs which had been discovered by previous writers on the subject, although they might be useful in identifying homosexuals who are emotionally disturbed enough to seek psychological assistance, were of no utility whatsoever when applied to matched groups of homosexuals and heterosexuals who were both socially well adjusted. Her work should stand as a distinct threat to those who rely upon the sign approach, whether these signs be personological or nosological.

In spite of all the cautions mentioned, the clinical psychologist should make his contribution to diagnosis whenever possible. If, on an empirical basis as well as a logical one, he finds that the pattern of test results is clearly reminiscent of a distinct type of personality disorder or other classifiable condition, he should so indicate toward the end of his report. However, he should take care that the body of the report is not comprised of rationalizations for the over-all halo effect that he perceives. The examiner should not feel obligated to make a diagnostic suggestion in those cases where the picture is not clear-cut.

Treatment Planning

Another focus may involve suggestions for the amelioration of the patient's difficulty through some environmental manipulation. This may consist of hospitalization accompanied by various kinds of treatment—intensive nursing care, tranquilization, electric or insulin coma therapy, individual or group psychotherapy, recreational and occupational therapy; or it may involve outpatient treatment either psychological, medical, or combined. Again, it may simply entail manipulating the individual's environment in some way which does not depend on his participation.

As mentioned, the usefulness of psychological reports for planning of this kind depends almost exclusively upon whether or not the referral problem is dealt with specifically and in detail. In an unpublished study by Suczek and myself carried on some years ago, the entire professional staff of an intensive treatment section of a neuropsychiatric hospital was asked to rate patients in terms of a number of personality variables following a detailed case discussion and presentation. It was discovered that interjudge reliability was only high on those items on which the consultant had made specific pronouncements and that otherwise everyone was largely on his own. The analogy is obvious. The psychologist's contribution to treatment planning will be minimal if the primary and secondary readers must carefully cull the elements of the report for some sort of vague hint or indication as to what the implications for treatment planning might be. He should be clear and to the point and, as much as possible, should make specific suggestions as to the implications of his findings. Psychological test results can be applied to an occupational therapy situation, a social casework situation, or any other situation in which people interact with one another. Certainly we know something about the relative efficiency of a given individual in structured and unstructured situations. We have some idea as to his relative degree of comfort with people of the same or opposite sex. We can make predictions about his reaction to authority figures or to peers and subordinates. When we can couch these findings in specific behavioral terms and translate them for the occupational therapist or group worker so that they can apply them in their own frame of reference, the patient stands to benefit considerably. Although, as Hammond and Allen have emphasized, the psychological report has secondary readers as well as primary ones, it may not be possible to focus on the needs of all these readers in a single written report. Sometimes it is necessary for the clinical psychologist to give additional verbal reports, each with its own focus, to his professional and subprofessional colleagues so that he can be maximally useful.

The focusing of psychological reports gains even greater importance now that psychologists feel freer than in the past to accept referrals from various, nontraditional sources. If the contribution of social workers, occupational therapists, and nurses to the care and treatment of the emotionally disturbed is to receive due recognition, there seems as much reason to accept requests for psychological evaluation directly from them as from medical colleagues.

Administrative Decisions

Frequently the psychologist is also asked to make specific suggestions concerning administrative decisions. These may involve the selection of workers, decisions about the status of patients in an institution, the promotion or separation of management personnel in industry, and similar selection tasks. Here the psychologist should be most cautious and circumspect in deciding whether to specify what the implications of a psychological test are concerning decisions of this kind. Since we know that total personality assessment has to be multilevel in nature, care must be taken that our psychological evaluations include multilevel assessment before making behavioral predictions. This is an important precaution since the question here is essentially one of prediction at the level of public communication, a level often not directly evaluated by the psychologist. It is perhaps for this reason that the Office of Strategic Services group, as it is described in *Assessment of Men* (26), had to resort to situational tests and to other direct measures of public behavior before the psychologists taking part in this mission felt free to make recommendations of this sort. If the psychologist's evaluation rests exclusively on projective instruments (level of private communication) and such tests as the Sentence Completion Test (level of conscious communication??), then perhaps he should make only contributions which would aid others in arriving at such decisions rather than attempt actual specific recommendations. Perhaps it is most ethical for the psychologist to emphasize the limitations of his instruments in this regard and to insist that either they be used only as a partial basis for the decision or that he be permitted to make assessment at other levels so as to arrive at an over-all recommendation which is justifiable. There is no reason whatsoever why the psychologist cannot be entrusted with the latter kind of responsibility, since the days of the "psychometrician" are certainly behind us.

Prediction of Other Behavior

For research or for clinical purposes the psychologist is sometimes asked to predict certain specific kinds of behavior. What happens in cases of this kind is illustrated by the study of Ullman, Berkman, and Hamister (27). Only to the extent that the psychologist is focused on the matter will he be useful. When the request is for specific predictions, it is best to use a battery containing operational measures of the variables under consideration, measures which, hopefully, have previously shown their predictive efficiency. Such a plan often involves an analysis of the behavior to be predicted into its components and a series of studies, including cross-validation, of ways of assessing or predicting this behavior. Many psychologists, particularly in industry, have developed excellent measures of specific kinds of behavior. The expectation that any psychological battery will make it possible for the skilled clinician to predict almost everything with accuracy is fallacious. The amount of certainty with which one can predict specific behavior depends upon the proved accuracy of the tool employed.

Summary

The importance of focusing the psychological report has been discussed. The body of the report should contain a thorough assessment of the individual insofar as justified by the tools employed. Toward the end of the report there should be a proposed solution to the dilemma posed by the referral, properly qualified as to the amount of certainty which is justified in the situation. Diagnostic and other kinds of signs have been discussed and found wanting in many respects. The role of the psychologist as a clinician rather than a psychometrist has been emphasized.

3
STYLE

MANY WRITERS feel that the style of the psychological report is vital in facilitating or complicating the process of communication. Hammond and Allen recommend a straight-forward expository style which emphasizes accuracy, integration, readability, and tone in preference to a quasi-literary style. They hold that misplaced modifiers, passive verbs, and indefinite references lead to ambiguity and should be assiduously avoided. In order to promote integration, they suggest a table of contents, an introductory summary, judiciously placed headings, parallel construction, numbered paragraphs, cross-references, paragraph organization, and so on. Whether the problem of communication is really as specifically grammatical as those suggestions imply is open to question.

Hammond and Allen recommend the elimination of superfluous words, the compression of thoughts, effective sentences of reasonable length, logical construction, and the utilization of intelligible punctuation to aid readability. The report, by taking an impersonal viewpoint, not addressing the reader directly, avoiding the introduction of irrevelant personalities, avoiding slang and colloquial expressions, and de-emphasizing the writer's own cognitive or perceptual processes, will achieve objectivity.

These authors seem to assume that if a set of rules can be followed in preparing a report, a style which more effectively communicates the findings to the referent will result.

This matter is approached from another direction by Austin Foster (9), who provides a few simple rules to guide the clinician in the style of his report. These include the elimination of technical "shop talk," the omission of names of specific tests, and the willingness of the psychologist to state explicitly that his findings do not make sense if such is the case.

The fact that style may influence communication is suggested by the following studies:

Forer (8) considers that the "personal" or "empirical" validation, as subjectively experienced by some clinical psychologists, is often due to the false security that they gain from the use of *universal* personality traits in their clinical reports and in their thinking. This false feeling of security is very similar to that gained by the interpretation of certain projective tests like the Szondi—interpretations made from this instrument are often so general and so universally applicable that almost any interpretation fits everyone. Forer gave a "test" to a group of students and then presented them with a set of interpretations or results which were all identical. Virtually all the students in this group felt that the interpretation was uniquely applicable to them. They rated the test as "very effective." (The paradigm used by Forer is very similar to that used in many studies carried on to assess the "validity" of tests. Since the students said that the results were applicable to them, Forer's test might be considered "valid.") In drawing implications for psychological reports, Forer suggests that if interpretations are couched in sufficiently palatable terms, it is no trick at all to impress some people. The implication is that psychologists should be wary of being misled by compliments from their colleagues in other professions. Perhaps their acceptance of psychological reports is due mainly to the smooth verbal techniques employed and not to any accuracy of interpretation or meaningful communication of findings. Most psychologists have listened at least once to an impressive literary display by a student which began with a conclusion and was subsequently rationalized beautifully, in textbook style, without any particular reference to the data upon which the report was presumably based.

Sundberg (23) matched actual interpretations of the Minnesota Multiphasic Personality Inventory with stereotyped interpretations which were faked. The subjects who had been given the test were supplied with pairs of interpretations, including their own and one of the stereotyped interpretations, and asked to select the one which best fitted their personality. The selection demonstrated no significant differences between the choices of real and faked interpretations. When these same pairs were shown to friends of the subjects they also were unable to detect the actual interpretations beyond chance expectancy. This study would tend to suggest that the criterion of personal validity has once again been brought into doubt. The results do not constitute a criticism of the MMPI, but of the ability of the psychologist to accurately, specifically and uniquely apply his findings to the particular subject and the particular situation. How this ability can be applied more effectively will be described in a later chapter.

Davenport (4) set herself the task of discovering statements based upon the Thematic Apperception Test which were non-ambiguous and discriminatory. A total of 207 statements were studied as to their reliability and discriminatory ability when applied to the protocols under consideration. In addition they were rated on a six-point ambiguity scale. It was discovered that many statements were universal, presumably indicating that the judges preferred not to be put on the spot or tied down. Although universal statements were quite frequent, ambiguous ones were not. This result seems to imply that ambiguity and universality, although both common phenomena, are not necessarily highly correlated. Most of the statements considered ambiguous were psychoanalytic in nature and many of those that were avoided were statements relating to personality assets. The results of this study illustrate the effect of the "maladjust-ment bias" (see Chapter 8) upon communication and emphasize the necessity for behavioral referents rather than for hypothet-ical constructs with which the reader might not agree.

Datel and Gengerelli (3) found that clinical psychologists were able to match individuals with Rorschach interpretations of colleagues beyond chance expectancy. Whether a criterion short of complete accuracy is a sufficient measure in this instance remains a moot point. The further suggestion by the authors that the heterogeneity of the group would tend to aid the accuracy of the matching procedure is in line with similar findings obtained in an unpublished study by the present writer. Clinical psychologists were asked to match Draw-A-Person and Rorschach protocols. It was found that this task could be done with great accuracy in a group which was heterogeneous as regards age, sex, and severity of maladjustment, but that the accuracy decreased sharply with increased homogeneity in respect to these variables. The implication is that the psychological report distinguishes one person from another when this distinction is easily made, but that it fails to do so when the group is seemingly homogeneous. This is an important indictment if true. In explaining their results, Datel and Gengerelli suggest (a) that tests are interpretated differently by different clinicians, (b) that they are reported differently, or what seems more likely, (c) that the reports are so ambiguous as to be non-discriminatory.

As Tallent (24) has pointed out, there are certain typical styles of reports:

The "Barnum" Style

Reports which contain universalities and ambiguities consist of a great deal of hoopla and very little substance. In such reports patients are almost inevitably described as having such characteristics as "difficulty in the expression of their instinctual drives," "some interpersonal difficulties," "a lack of full integration or self-actualization," "potential intelligence considerably higher than their present functioning efficiency," and so forth. Such statements are all mildly derogatory or subtly flattering and tend to be applicable to almost anyone at all in a matching procedure like that used by Sundberg. Use of this type of report would probably be a great temptation to clinical psychologists acting as consultants to top management in industry. Such consultants, therefore, will have to struggle with special vigor in order to withstand the temptation of becoming a psychological P. T. Barnum.

The "Aunt Fanny" Style

This type of report, so aptly styled by Tallent, is one that contains information that is true of everyone, including every man's "Aunt Fanny." Even though most clinical psychologists would deny that their report ever conformed to this stereotype, none can deny the presence of *some* "Aunt Fanny" kinds of statements in almost every psychological report. How many have not at one time or another described a given patient as having "latent homosexuality," "masturbatory anxiety," "a conflict between dependence and independence," "some anxiety," "some impairment of intellectual efficiency," "immaturity," "some inconsistency of affective reactions," "an inability to express his aggressive and hostile impulses," "some difficulty with people in authority as well as those of the opposite sex," and so on *ad nauseum*? Here it might be asked "Is there a man with soul so dead who never to himself hath said, 'Don't I possess all of these characteristics—and so does my Aunt Fanny'" (with apologies to Sir Walter Scott and Norman Tallent).

The "Madison Avenue" Report

Unfortunately, some clinical psychologists utilize this kind of a report as a way of solving their interpersonal difficulties. Some years ago I had the experience of overhearing a psychologist say to a psychiatrist following a heated discussion of a case at a staff conference: "I agree with you, Dr. Blank. And I will give some psychological tests to show that you are right." The implications of this statement are obvious. The psychologist in question, in attempting to ingratiate himself with his medical colleagues, used the psychological examination as an excuse for offering a set of rationalizations designed not to communicate his findings but to "sell a bill of goods at any price." Many clinical psychologists do likewise for more socially acceptable reasons than the one just mentioned. For instance, a beginning psychologist, upon discovering that someone is a homosexual, may carefully search the psychological test data for "signs of homosexuality," whatever these may be. His report may contain a choice description of the classical dynamics of homosexuality which may be more or less efficiently rationalized on the basis of the test data, depending upon how skillful the clinical psychologist is in rationalizing. In his zeal for clarity, the clinical psychologist may overlook much data which would also be pertinent and helpful in evaluating the patient. Furthermore, he may focus upon aspects of the patient's pathology and areas of his personality which are relatively tangential and irrelevant.

This type of report may also take its cue from a negative kind of motivation. Perhaps the referent feels that the patient has organic brain damage, schizophrenia, or some other condition whose presence the clinical psychologist is inclined to deny for some reason or another. His report may then constitute an all-out effort to disprove the hypothesis of the referent. Entire psychological reports devoted to the argument that the patient under study does *not* have a certain condition seem rather pointless. The question concerning patients is what they have rather than what they do not have; information as to the patient's existing characteristics is what is needed to help in his evaluation and treatment. However, the "Madison Avenue" report, regardless of whether it is meant to placate someone or to serve as an expression of hostility, seems to have little utility.

The Scientific Report

The scientific report should have a style which emphasizes accuracy, integration, and readability as described by Hammond and Allen. In addition it should emphasize clarity and individuality as emphasized by Forer, Tallent, Foster, and many others. The "Aunt Fanny" types of statements need not be entirely dispensed with, but they certainly have to be greatly individualized before they communicate much of value. For example, it would be very helpful to the referent if the concept of homosexuality could be discussed in terms of the level at which it appears in a given patient, the amount of difficulty it is causing him, his conscious reaction to it, the way it manifests itself in overt behavior, and to what extent it has become an interpersonal and intrapsychic problem to him. All that can really be salvaged from the "Madison Avenue" report is a description of the reasons for arriving at a certain diagnostic conclusion. It goes without saying that the personality description should lead logically to whatever diagnostic conclusions the clinical psychologist may draw. The evidence cited should be of a theoretical and empirical sort, but certainly not test-bound. In other words, when the clinical psychologist concludes that the patient is schizophrenic, he should emphasize such features as confusion of thought processes, disassociation, personality disintegration, and shallowness of affect rather than low F+ per cent, high Sc scale, or a certain Wechsler pattern.

Needless to say, the usual rules of politeness and courtesy hold in a psychological report as elsewhere. Care should be taken to avoid a condescending or defensive manner when addressing or referring to professional colleagues. Such statements as "in spite of the psychiatrist's findings," "contrary to the recommendations of the social worker," or "contrary to what might be supposed by the school principal," certainly do not facilitate the processes of communication.

Summary

Style was discussed and reference was made to some clear-cut suggestions by Hammond and Allen as to how the application of certain basic rules of English could greatly improve the psychological report. A number of studies indicating that style is very much a problem and that improvement of style facilitates communication were reviewed. Certain typical styles were discussed and a bias in favor of the scientific report which emphasizes accuracy, lack of ambiguity, individuality, and objectivity was expressed.

4
ORGANIZATION

ONE OF THE most crucial issues in the area of psycho-logical report writing is that of organization. I once went over the report of a student I was supervising for the first time. After groping through a labyrinth of unrelated data, only to end up with a rather well-organized and concise summary, I asked the student to explain himself. He replied that since no one would read anything but the summary anyway, he felt there was little use in attempting to impose a stricter organization upon the remainder of the report. It is in the matter of organization that the sophisticated clinical psychologist and the beginner most clearly betray themselves. Those who have inadequate understanding of personality or pathology frequently organize their report in a way which gives the impression that the tests are the object of investigation rather than the client himself. In this chapter an attempt is made to review critically some of the common forms of organization and to evaluate their assets and liabilities.

Theory-Oriented Report

Although relatively rare, this kind of psychological report deserves special consideration. It is illustrated, for example, by Behn (1) writing for a German publication. Discussing the need for adequate communication and reminding the psychologist that he deals with probabilities rather than certainties, Behn goes on to say that it is always safe to specify the constitutional type of the individual. This recommendation is modified by the suggestion that patients being described are not always consistent as to type. Metaphysical explanations are considered unnecessary, but it is considered appropriate to always relate the constitutional type to the temperamental type of the individual. By the use of correlations Behn considers it possible to produce a full report from minimal data. Different words are suggested to give the flavor of an adaptive-maladaptive continuum. The whole scheme smacks of a combination of pseudo-scientific typology followed by "arty" free association.

While to the American reader this might seem unnecessarily esoteric and too unusual to be worthy of mention, there exist home-grown variations of the same kind of theoretical over-emphasis in psychological reports. There is, for example, the would-be psychoanalyst among clinical psychologists whose report seeks to detail the stages of psychosexual development, the esoterica of the oedipal involvement, the free flow of the libido hither and yon, and concludes finally that a great deal of uncovering is necessary to bring the repressed material to awareness before the individual can be properly evaluated, to say nothing of being relieved of his pathology. Then there is the clinical psychologist who feels that in order to retain his identity as a scientist it is necessary to couch his psychological report in terms of learning theory. Instead of psychotherapy he refers to retraining, instead of the environment he refers to external stimuli, while various kinds of behavior on the part of the patient become responses.

Illustrative of such writing is the following student's psycho-analytically-oriented report on a 32-year-old woman suffering from anorexia nervosa.

Tests Administered

Rorschach
Thematic Apperception Test
Draw-A-Person
House-Tree-Person

Behavior During Examination

This patient was quite seductive during the administration of the psychological tests. Her apparent distaste for the examiner only served to cover up her basically erotic attitude towards the opposite sex. Her incessant smoking and requests for a drink indicated her oral pre-occupation under stress, whereas the sparsity of her preformance symbolized her anal retentiveness. All in all, her behavior was mainly pregenital in nature.

Analysis of Test Data

The patient's present way of adjusting is basically due to the domination of the pleasure principle which makes it difficult for her to think in long-range terms and produces behavior designed to meet the immediate satisfactions of the moment. She has never been able to cathect love objects beyond the narcissistic stage because of a weakness in ego development. The only effect of the anal period upon her personality is a tendency to be negativistic and rebellious, as manifested symptomatically by her unwillingness to partake of oral succourance in a manner common to others.

Her present difficulties can also be traced to the presence of certain tendencies towards sexual perversion which can be found in her fantasy. A preoccupation with the possibility of fellatio probably prevents her from enjoying normal oral pleasures. Her defenses of isolation and projection, in addition to the basic repressive techniques, make further uncovering of her conflicts difficult, but not impossible. Intensive therapy over a long period of time would seem to be a "must."

In evaluating a report of this kind one must consider not only its ability to communicate to a variety of readers, but also its unique contribution to the understanding of a patient. Obviously organization must be in terms that are acceptable to the primary reader as well as to the greatest majority of secondary readers possible. If material such as that described above can actually be inferred from psychological tests, it can probably be deduced with greater ease by an analyst in the same length of time. In addition to theoretical inconsistencies, the report describes the patient only in broad outline and tells little about her psychic content. It appears that the writer of the report may have used (or abused) the psychological test data to justify his sterotype of such a person which in turn he may have derived from an entirely different source.

Test-Oriented Report

This form of report is usually organized to emphasize sources of information and discusses in some detail how the interpretations were derived. Two sets of reasons are usually given for this procedure.

1. The need from a *training* standpoint: This objective implies that the sole basis that the supervisor has for evaluating

the diagnostic work of a psychology trainee is his written report. Consequently, in a medical setting communication to the entire staff, including the primary and secondary readers, would then be sacrificed for the sake of training. The efficiency of this kind of training is to be seriously questioned. Later, a method will be suggested for greatly improving training and for relieving the psychological report of the burden of responsibility for communication between student and supervisor along with the many other chores it is asked to perform.

2. The need for citing *"evidence"* (not to be confused with using test data for illustration): A number of interesting assumptions underlie the supposed need of the clinical psychologist to substantiate his conclusions by citing "test evidence." The first assumption is that the predictive qualities of psychological tests are so obvious that anyone will be able to see from the description of a given test phenomenon that the behavioral analogy suggested or the clinical diagnosis made follows inevitably. The second assumption is that the clinical psychologist's interpretations are bound to be suspected unless he can somehow document and substantiate them, in spite of the fact that members of other professions apparently do not feel the need to substantiate their findings with concrete kinds of evidence. When, for example, the psychiatrist speaks of shallow affect he expects that his colleagues will concede him sufficient clinical judgment and professional sensitivity to make such a statement without having to cite specific incidents to substantiate his views. When the social worker reports to the staff that the economic status of the home is borderline, she is not expected to specify in detail what is and is not in the home in support of her interpretation. It is difficult to understand the motives underlying the psychologist's need to assume that he must document his interpretations. One motive is undoubtedly his desire to impress other people. In this connection, he may need to overcome feelings of insecurity and inadequacy in a medical setting by citing what he deems to be "scientific" evidence favoring his particular interpretation.

It is pointed out by Hammond and Allen (12) that the psychological findings should be presented as a coherent whole. In selecting materials for presentation, the irrelevant and insignificant should be omitted. By way of emphasis, they explicitly state that reporting psychological data test by test in conformity with the examination sequence seems insulting to the reader because of its extremely nonfunctional nature. Foster (9) agrees that a test by test discussion in the report is quite unnecessary and nonfunctional. The same point of view is also made explicit by Palmer (18), who criticizes the test-oriented report on the grounds that the concept of the test as a sample of behavior of the particular individual under study is seldom in evidence. He points out that this kind of report often abounds in redundancies. Integration does not take place until the summary, and then the argument is often inconclusive. Palmer contends that this kind of organization magnifies the threat of "halo" effect because of the possibility of biasing the interpretation of one test so that it merges with the interpretations of others. Palmer points out that test-oriented reports are not restricted merely to those in which the name of the test heads each section, sometimes this organization is implicit. In its most extreme form, a different paragraph or section is devoted to a specific part of the test. Thus there might be a paragraph dealing with the psychogram evaluation of the Rorschach and other paragraphs based on the interpretation of each ratio and percentage. Each and every TAT story might similarly receive separate paragraphs. Such reports deal only with very concrete interpretations of test scores or data and fail to generalize as to their meaning for the patient in question. They unfortunately characterize the work of many inadequately trained clinical psychologists and tend to misrepresent the psychological profession to many segments of the public.

In defense of the "test evidence" approach, Holzberg, Alessi and Wexler state that the body of the report should be concerned with the concrete evidence, the interpretations, and the generalizations. Lodge (17) feels that the nature of the evidence on which each statement is based should be included at all times. Palmer lists as one of the advantages of this approach the focus it gives to the different contributions of the several tests and their seeming incongruities. If the projective tests were sorted and hierarchically arranged according to levels of awareness, the reader would then be more aware of the personality characteristics at each level and the degree of integration present or absent.

The following illustration is the report of a 37-year-old woman referred for a psychological evaluation in order to obtain information concerning a differential diagnosis and "dynamics pertinent to treatment."

General Observations

The patient is a tall, rather attractive, well-groomed woman of 37. Even before entering the examination room she began talking rapidly and continued throughout the ensuing three hours except when interrupted by the examiner and given a specific task to perform. In manic-like fashion her speach was very dramatic, she waved her arms, and laughed inappropriately. Her verbalizations were somewhat tangenital and the topics were generally irrelevant and quickly changing.

Test Interpretation

On the verbal subtests of the WAIS, which were administered for possible diagnostic cues, the patient was found to be functioning in an inconsistent manner. Her scores ranged from the superior to the dull normal level of ability, partly because of her general negativistic behavior and tendency to give up very easily on tasks such as arithmetic problems. This inconsistency was also displayed in the contrast between the superior quality of some of her answers and the rather bizarre quality of others (e.g., "an eye and an ear are alike because they are all accoustics of the body, openings in the body").

Similarly, on a self-descriptive sentence-completion test the patient's perceptions of herself as being unhappy, nervous, dependent on her family, unconventional and unwilling to do what is expected of her, were in contrast to other much less insightful statements. Thus, while to one test item she responded "I hate people—and yet in my heart I feel I really don't, they only make me nervous," she went on to refer to most women as "bitches" and to men as "beasts."

The patient's responses to the unstructured Rorschach material were markedly childish ("cute little pussy cats"), autistically toned, and inconsistent. At times the accuracy of her percepts was good and at other times poor; likewise on some occasions she was very productive, only to suddenly become markedly constricted for no discernible external cause. Her productivity was manifested only in her attention to many small insignificant details, analogous to her "manic-like" behavior described above.

Several of her responses were anatomical and sexual in content, suggesting a preoccupation with sexual matters. These percepts poorly matched the stimuli qualities and approached the bizarreness seen in a psychotic processes. When asked routinely to elaborate on a percept, the patient became defensive about the sexual ones and shifted the responsibility for them to the examiner by saying that he forced her to re-examine the cards closely, denying that she had ever had such thoughts before.

The patient's scores on objective personality tests indicated a high manifest anxiety (to a degree rarely or never found in any but psychiatric patients), as well as felt needs for compulsive orderliness and for restriction or guidance from others (exclusive of any close interpersonal relationships). At the same time her need for change, for new experiences, and for a widening of acquaintances, fell short of that of 99 per cent of healthy women, a poor prognostic sign.

Summary

The test performance emphasized the patient's varied ability and inefficiency in spite of an above-average intellectual potential and productivity. Atypical ideation and perceptions, negativism and rebellious needs for economy, compulsive preoccupation with irrelevant details, and social relationships maintained by rationalization, projection, and denial were also indicated. These test results suggested most nearly a diagnosis of schizophrenia, schizo-affective type.

A report of this kind makes it very difficult to understand the patient described because of the discreteness of the observations which in turn are devoid of any etiologic sequence or adequate abstractions concerning personality traits. This material has relatively little meaning to those unfamiliar with the tests described; for those who are familiar with them it will not be necessary to discuss the findings in this way. The raw test data may sometimes be useful for illustrative purposes, but it is no substitute for interpretation.

Problem-Oriented Report

This kind of report is sharply focused on the particular question asked by the referent, if there is one. This focus is certainly in line with Hammond and Allen's suggestion that reports be functional, adapted to the reader, and that irrelevant material be omitted. Such a report is preferred by many referents to the stereotyped "dynamically oriented" report which inevitably discusses all facets of the personality and pathology of the individual, leaving the reader in doubt as to the psychologist's opinion on the vital issue at hand. Holzberg et al. point out that in most clinical settings it is not always possible or desirable to engage in extensive testing, since evaluation must be confined to the exploration of those areas specifically related to the referral problem. Aware that the staff conference may, embarrassingly, raise issues not adequately covered in the psychological report, these authors advocate stating clearly the limitations of the study as laid down by the original referral.

Palmer (18) points out two possible sources of bias inherent in the problem-oriented report. First, evaluation and discussion may be limited to the particular question posed, neglecting other aspects of the individual's functioning, thus not only limiting the contribution of the tests employed but also failing to fully utilize the resources inherent in the battery. Furthermore, it may lead to the neglect of etiologic hypotheses and the interrelatedness of the individual's difficulties with other aspects of his behavior. Second, such a report may reflect theoretical biases of the referent, the institution, or the clinician in favor of organic etiology, functional etiology, or the favorite use of certain nosological classifications, to name a few. Instead, Palmer feels that it is the psychologist's ethical obligation, as part of his teaching duty, to promote a consideration of all possible viewpoints.

These limitations are exemplified by the following report on a patient referred by a physician in a state hospital because he was thought to be mentally defective. The test findings indicated that he was not mentally defective, but suffered instead from severe schizophrenic symptoms. All that was stated in the psychological report, however, was the following:

Tests Administered

> Wechsler-Bellevue, Form I
> Bender-Gestalt
> Wechsler Memory Scale
> Rorschach

Behavior During Examination

During the examination the patient was confused, distracted, and continuously on the move. Sometimes he answered the questions put to him and sometimes he did not. Some of the things he said sounded rather peculiar.

Analysis of Tests

The patient received an IQ of 95 on the Wechsler-Bellevue, indicating that he is of at least average intelligence. He performed best on the Information, Comprehension, and Digit Symbol subtests, but did quite poorly on Arithmetic and Block Design. His highest weighted subtest score was 14 and his lowest was 5. His memory appears somewhat deficient as defined by a WMS Memory Quotient of only 78. The Rorschach indicates some confusion but also contains many signs of average ability.

I am opposed to the problem-oriented report in this extreme form. The first assumption usually made by writers of this kind of report is that those outside the profession of clinical psychology who frequently make referrals are sufficiently spohisticated about the testing resources of the psychologist to use the report effectively and appropriately. No familiarity obtained from a general orientation to clinical psychology such as is commonly supplied in medical school or graduate social work school curriculums is equivalent to the thorough training of the psychologist. The problem as stated by the referent is merely his guess concerning one of the paths that might fruitfully be explored by the psychologist. The referent may be no more capable of accurately predicting the psychologist's contribution than the psychologist is capable of predicting the effects of specific drugs although he has had courses in chemistry and physiology.

It should be remembered at all times that the competent psychologist can best be utilized as a clinical consultant. What is wanted from him is a professional judgment based upon whatever tools he chooses to employ. If the examiner is a trainee in clinical psychology, confidence is presumedly being placed in the judgment of his supervisor who should be a competent, qualified clinical psychologist. If the function is being performed by someone who is neither fully qualified nor supervised, then the full resources of the profession are not being employed and the results will be correspondingly inferior.

It is somewhat of an ethical problem as to what the clinical psychologist should do if when evaluating an individual thought to have purely intellectual difficulties, he discovers a serious personality disorder. Certainly it should be brought to the attention of some responsible party and perhaps psychiatric evaluation or a more complete psychological evaluation can be recommended. Very few people would tell an internist what to look for or insist that he restrict his findings to a particular area. When exploratory surgery is suggested, it is difficult to know what will come up. Legal advice from an experienced and qualified attorney often reveals new developments. Business consultants may come up with original and creative suggestions which exceed the limits of the particular problem referred to them. If the psychologist regresses to the role of laboratory technician or psychometrician and his reports consist merely of the scores derived from tests, he is neglecting his responsibility and is harming both the patient and the profession. A mature clinical psychologist always views his task of evaluation as a global one. In other words, although focusing on the problem raised by the referent is in order, restricting the report to this particular problem is out of order. The ethical code of the psychologist states that his ultimate responsibility is to society and to the welfare of the client. To merely report the intelligence quotient of a child who, in the opinion of the psychologist, is schizophrenic, does not meet this ethical criterion.

Personality-Area Oriented Reports

This type of organization focuses upon the patient rather than the sources of information.

Hammond and Allen stress the crucial importance of adapting the report to the reader and meeting his particular needs for functional information. They suggest that particular emphasis be given to a statement of purpose and that the summary appear at the outset rather than at the end. They imply that a report should always be organized with the reader's limitations and his ability to carry out recommendations in mind. Sometimes one report will simply not suffice for all the various purposes implied in the referral. When a child is evaluated, a written report which can be made generally available to educational personnel may go to the school. This report might be very brief, serving only as a record that the evaluation has indeed been completed, and containing little specific information. An oral report to the teacher herself may focus upon what can be done within the classroom setting to aid the child with his particular problems. There is little value in providing the teacher with recommendations governing the relationship between the child and its parents or the care of the child in the home. By the same token a report to the mother, again preferably oral in nature, should focus upon her contribution to the child's welfare and adjustment. Making recommendations to her about the schoolroom situation may well lead to nothing more than increased ill-will between home and school which would certainly not rebound to the benefit of the child-client.

Palmer refers to this form of report organization as the "patient-oriented" study. He suggests that the report begin with a summary of the patient's outstanding overt and covert characteristics, followed by a detailed description of his manifest behavior. He urges careful attention to the distinction between the patient's surface traits and his underlying adaptive techniques of control. To Palmer, the two main features of this kind of report are the focus on the patient rather than on the tests and its theoretical consistency and comprehensibility. This approach is designed to give maximum attention to the description and explanation of the patient's behavior, unbound by either the tools employed or the practical limitations of the situation. Theories and hypotheses need not be omitted because of their lack of finality, but may be brought out in this context without being clothed in a false mantle of certainty.

Illustrations of this kind of report are to be found in the appendix.

Ego-Psychological Reports

A kind of report in line with modern psychological theory is the ego-psychological report first discussed by Bellak (2). This report, more than any other, takes into account the necessity for focus upon the assets and strengths of the individual in coping with life's demands, deviating from the traditional tendency to emphasize pathology. In ego psychology it is assumed that fantasy has adaptive properties and is not just a safety valve for frustrated drives. Consequently, much of the material derived from projective techniques can be analyzed in terms of its adaptive value rather than merely in terms of conflict areas uncovered against the will of the patient. In this system the level tapped by a particular projective instrument is specified and analyzed and a continuum from the latent to the manifest is established for both diagnostic and prognostic purposes. Since the ego is considered to have a regulating and ordering function which permits adjustment in spite of all the difficulties involved, it is seen as the main intervening variable between the test data and the inferred behavior, both present and predictable. Pathological indications are then considered as ego-defects and their organic or functional origin becomes relatively tangential. Looseness and flexibility (regression in the service of the ego) can be differentiated clearly from helplessness and flaccidity in dealing with complex and stressful situations.

Such a report always focuses upon an analysis of the defenses, not only in terms of their presence or absence, but in terms of their adequacy or inadequacy in bringing about more effective interpersonal behavior. No interpretations are made without clear awareness of the stimulus as well as of the organism in producing a final response. The report always contains a thorough description of the underlying needs and personality structure of the individual while not neglecting his conception of himself and the world about him, both in conscious terms and, if possible, in behavioral ones. An example follows from the report on a 29-year-old woman with marital problems, referred to determine more precisely the nature of her difficulties and the severity of her emotional disturbance.

Behavior During Examination

The patient was deferential and cooperative during the examination, readily complying with all that was asked of her. She became quite tense and anxious from time to time, but seemed to relax as the examination progressed.

Report of Test Findings

This patient's major difficulty is that she cannot see herself consistently. Sometimes she regards herself as an object of deprivation and hostility, whereas at other times she conceives of herself as sinful, vicious and cruel to those about her. She has a need to express her aggression and sometimes succeeds, but never without suffering a sharp guilt reaction.

Her anal needs are very pronounced, manifesting themselves in excessive orderliness, perfectionism, and almost constant preoccupation with small sums of money. Her oral behavior is mainly aggressive and sadistic and one can easily see why her husband finds it rather difficult to live with her from time to time. Paternal figures are seen as unyielding and cold, whereas women—particularly maternal figures—are sources of conflict because of their inconsistent seductiveness and tendency to reject.

Her main conflicts center around the direction of her aggression, whether it be expressed toward herself or toward others, and the desire to maintain her anal rituals against the threat of being disturbed in the process.

Although compulsive defenses are employed, they do not seem to be totally successful and the mechanism of projection is constantly coming to the fore. Basically she seems very narcissistic and consequently is unable to give any real warmth or affection to those about her. The strong desire to replicate her relationship with her father has made it very difficult for her to get much gratification from her present heterosexual contact with her husband.

In spite of all the difficulties this woman is experiencing, her ego strength is amazingly well retained. Her behavior as judged from the psychological tests is rational and there are only very sporatic indications of weakening ties to reality. Her ability to compartmentalize her difficulties enables her to go from day-to-day without bearing the increasing burden of the accumulating failures she seems to be experiencing because of her inability to meet the needs of others. The dynamic picture is consistent with a borderline schizophrenic condition with quite favorable prognosis.

Review of Organizational Schemes

There are as many specific organizational schemes as people who have suggested them. An excellent review of some utilized in various agencies was conducted by Hammond and Allen (pp. 186-231). Palmer's scheme first lists sources of information, followed by sections devoted to "test behavior observations," the analysis of results, and finally the summary. Palmer lists the tests under sources of information without citing any particular test data. "Observations" has reference to the patient, his behavior, and attitudes during various portions of the examination, especially insofar as they may throw light upon the patient's differential reactions to various stimuli and affect the representativeness of the test results and their interpretation. The section on analysis of results is an attempt to communicate a description of the patient's functioning as well as to make guesses as to the possible source or genesis of his behavior patterns. In the summary the intention is not merely to restate data already made explicit, but rather to derive from the preceding descriptions a set of conclusions and inferences concerning the patient's behavior. Here he returns to the central theme which has been stated at the outset. Palmer also strongly recommends an oral discussion with the referent as a supplement to the written report.

The report outline suggested by Holzberg, Alessi, and Wexler is very similar to that just described, with sections devoted to "reason for the referral," "behavioral observations," a "data analysis" and "conclusions." However, the main difference lies in the special attention given to intelligence in a separate section, the contention being that the patient's intelligence should serve as a frame of reference within which to interpret the results of the other tests. This argument seems to overlook the fact that intelligence test results may reflect more the patient's current pathology than provide a frame of reference for comprehending it.

Hammond and Allen suggest beginning with a "statement of purpose" and an "opening summary," then having a carefully executed plan, tailor-made for the specific needs of the situation. They strongly recommend drawing up an outline before actually writing the report.

A very detailed description of how to write a psychological report is presented by Lodge (17). He offers suggestions as to actual time-limits for the various phases of the job, suggestions as to what kind of a pencil to use, the judicious use of scratch paper, the length of the sentences, and when to submit the report for supervision. While this kind of syllabus might have had its use at one time, it seems rather inadequate for our current purposes.

5
A NEW WAY OF ORGANIZING PSYCHOLOGICAL REPORTS

PSYCHOLOGISTS training interns and practicum students have long been impressed by the need for well-organized psychological reports and by the varied problems presented in the training situation by report-writing. The following method was developed in an attempt to solve some of the problems.

PREPARATION OF OUTLINE

When a trainee is assigned a patient for evaluation, together with his supervisor, he chooses a test battery on the basis of whatever information is available. His choice is dictated in part by what is known of the predictive efficiency of various instruments and in part by clinical folklore as to what test is most appropriate for a particular kind of patient. The trainee is asked to defend each instrument chosen, usually leading to the statement and discussion of some rather interesting hypotheses. The supervisor emphasizes that such plans for diagnostic testing are necessarily tentative and explicitly instructs the trainee to do a complete evaluation of the patient, changing his test battery as he goes along or the situation may dictate, since it is difficult to predict with any assurance whether a patient will reveal important material in response to a particular set of stimuli. The outcome of testing may depend upon the interpersonal situation arising between examiner and patient as well as upon many other transient situational variables and the examiner must retain sufficient flexibility of approach to insure a thorough investigation.

The trainee is instructed to score all of the tests, following which he is to begin his analysis of the data. For the purpose of listing his hypotheses he is supplied with the outline form shown

Tests administered	Bender-Gestalt	WAIS	Rorschach	MMPI	TAT	Sentence Completion
Behavior during test						
Intellectual aspects of the personality						
Affective aspects of the personality						
Basic conflict areas						
Adaptive and maladaptive techniques						
Diagnostic indicators						
Prognostic implications						

in table 1. The boxes along the left describe various areas of focus. The student is asked to write at least one statement in every box if possible. This alerts him to the necessity of carefully evaluating the data he has collected and prompts him to cull as many interpretative hypotheses as possible. These hypotheses are presumably at the highest possible level of inference. In supervision one frequently finds that students are capable of deriving much more information from the tests than ever finds its way into the report.

To guide the student in determining whether an hypothesis belongs in one or the other horizontal category, they are carefully defined as indicated below. Illustrative test material may be included on the form, but can also be presented verbally during the supervisory session. The outline form is on extra-large (legal-size) paper, since ordinary 8½" x 11" paper is too small. The trainee is encouraged to be as daring as possible in listing his various hypotheses on the grounds that his thinking can best be evaluated and refined by making it thoroughly explicit, thereby providing material for full discussion in the supervisory session. He is particularly encouraged to exploit each instrument separately so that seeming inconsistencies and incongruities in the patient's personality become evident in all their complexity. All too often psychologists tend to play down the skill necessary in diagnostic testing. Any psychologist who makes a real effort to exploit a test battery finds that psychodiagnostic testing is one of the most complex and difficult jobs imaginable that requires all his resources. The areas of focus are defined as follows:

Behavior During Examination

This section contains a report of the patient's behavior during the examination in each stimulus situation. Since the concept of "establishing rapport" is too vague to be of any great value in individual assessment, the psychologist is asked instead to specify the patient's behavior towards him, the circumstances of the examination, and other pertinent stimuli which may either modify test interpretations or be of predictive value on their own. It seems important to list the behavior in each stimulus situation separately because of the variation in the amount of structure from one test to the next. The importance of the stimulus in guiding behavior in a semistructured situation such as that provided by a projective test must be emphasized. Some patients seem most competent when a great deal of structure is provided. They seem delighted with the WAIS and, to a lesser extent, with the MMPI and the Sentence-Completion Test, but with the presentation of the TAT and the Rorschach they become disenchanted with the procedure and begin to feel ill at ease. On the other hand, there are those patients who can only be comfortable when allowed to react in the most idiosyncratic manner imaginable. Their discomfort increases as structure becomes more and more a part of the stimulus situation. Also valuable is a comparison of the patient's subjective discomfort with his objective success on each test, providing a clue to how realistic is his self-concept. Where reality ties are still fairly intact, subjective discomfort is apt to parallel objective inefficiency, but where reality is misperceived, as in the schizophrenic, minimal affective display may accompany maximal inefficiency. This particular section may also contain predictions concerning the patient's characteristic ways of responding to failure and success. Such behavior is certainly of great import in determining stress-tolerance, the ability to adjust to various job situations, and over-all ego strength.

The interpersonal relationship between examiner and patient as it varies throughout the psychological examination is a rich source of interpretative hypotheses. Needless to say, it is not justifiable to assume that all the hostility displayed by a patient during an examination is a result of his pathology. It may be that the examiner is somehow not functioning at optimal efficiency at any given time toward a particular person. It is therefore helpful to make the trainee aware of his own role in evoking responses from patients so that in making his test interpretations he may learn to isolate that which is due to the examiner. It is important for him to carefully examine and identify his reactions toward the patient so as to have a basis for making general predictions about the patient's social stimulus value. Some of the test situations involve considerably more interaction than others and the patient may react differentially, depending upon the degree to which he feels comfortable with his dependency or affiliative needs as opposed to his desire to be independent or isolated.

Also contained in this section of the outline are verbal statements made by the patient regarding the various assessment procedures, statements which may not be scorable but which nevertheless have important implications. By making these explicit during the supervisory session it may often be possible to sensitize the trainee to important clues which he would otherwise tend to gloss over and not take sufficiently into account in his over-all evaluation. Many trainees find themselves capable of making a great many pertinent observations of this kind which often add substantially to the total apperceptive mass concerning the individual patient under consideration. For instance, a patient's insistence that the WAIS performance tests are childish and that his children could therefore do much better on them may greatly influence his performance. It may also reflect discomfort with his own inability to successfully compete with even such subordinate figures as children. Such behavior demonstrates the ego's role in defending against feelings of inadequacy and insecurity by utilizing the "sour grapes" technique. Or again, when in response to the Rorschach a patient continually requests the "correct" answer in spite of frequent reassurances that there is no such "correct" answer, it may reduce the number of responses to the test. It also gives the impression of extreme suspiciousness and lack of faith in both himself and the environment and focuses upon the inability of the ego to successfully cope with unsystematic irregularity and ambiguity. Likewise, in dealing with expressive techniques such as the Bender-Gestalt and the Draw-A-Person, the patient may produce many seemingly gratuitous associations whose symbolic value will become obvious on careful scrutiny.

Equally important are various reactions reflecting the patient's current pathology and preoccupations. These may be verbal in nature, taking the form of actual hallucinatory or delusional material, or else serving as the basis from which pathology may be indirectly inferred. Frequent requests for reassurance lead the examiner to predict over-dependency; frequent criticisms of the test may reveal the patient's characteristic method of expressing hostility, showing how he arouses anxiety and antagonism in those about him. There may also be non-verbal expressions of pathology in the form of belching, wandering about, excessive perspiration, nail biting, and so on. Here as elsewhere the student is asked not to list such pieces of behavior discretely but to make appropriate interpretations and predictions.

Intellectual Aspects of Personality

A person's intellectual efficiency is an important consideration in evaluating the kind of treatment that might prove most efficacious in rehabilitating him. All too often statements about intellectual efficiency are based exclusively upon the over-all intelligence test results, in spite of the fact that intellectual estimates are also derived from other tests in the battery. Because this outline encourages discussion of each test separately in terms of the patient's functioning efficiency in various areas, variations in performance between tests are quickly noticed. If a patient demonstrates much greater efficiency on intelligence tests than on the Rorschach or the TAT, this may signify that because of his ego-weakness his efficiency decreases as there are fewer guides and less positive feedback. There is also the possibility that a certain rebelliousness and negativism inherent in the patient's present behavoir results in motivational variability within the more structured situation, leading to inefficiency in this medium.

There is much reference in psychological reports to "intellectual potential" and how it is presumed to differ from current efficiency. Sometimes such terms as "capacity" and "ability" only further confuse the issue. When potential is mentioned often no distinction is made between potential which might have been present at the outset of life and which may no longer be present and potential which can result in increased efficiency within the near future as a result of psychiatric treatment. It is almost a truism in psychological report writing to say that the patient's efficiency is lower than his potential. By carefully scrutinizing the results of each test and differentially reporting them on this outline form, it may be possible to pin down the elusive matter of potential. If potential is gauged from intelligence test data it may be necessary to question whether the inconsistency of performance is sufficiently great to warrant the hypothesis. On the other hand, if potential is gauged from the Rorschach, a scrutiny of the recent literature may be advisable to check whether the criteria used are really appropriate. Further research with the TAT may demonstrate whether the structuring of the stories yield important clues to intelligence, although this test has not yet been used for this purpose. If some real difference between potential and current efficiency seems in evidence, the trainee should offer some hypotheses as to the reason for the difference. Certainly a vague statement that "the patient is unable to function at his potential because of emotional problems" is inadequate and hardly very useful. Instead it is desirable to specify the particular conditions accompanying inefficiency. These may involve ambiguity, pressure, interpersonal situations with specific kinds of persons (same or opposite sex, the same or a different age, etc.), or it may be due to a transient or irreversible impairment or deterioration.

Another important personality area which can be discussed under this category is that of level of aspiration—what a patient aspires to beyond his present ability to achieve. He may aspire to greater abstractions, as demonstrated by consistent attempts to generalize or organize in ways that are forced or otherwise inefficient; he may aspire to greater specificity and accuracy than he can achieve, manifested by an excessively picayune approach on the Bender, Rorschach, or TAT. Aspirations may be constructive forces leading to future achievements of great magnitude or they may be a helpless defense against probable failure in real situations. A good example of how an excessive or inappropriate aspiration level may become a part of the patient's pathology is given in the Case of Mike in Chapter 9.

The range of his interests is also of frequent significance in the patient's intellectual makeup. Probably the most direct evidence for range of interest comes from vocational interest inventories such as the Strong and Kuder. Whether diversity of content on the Rorschach can lead to accurate predictions in this regard has never really been definitively investigated, but certainly the variety of themes generated by the TAT and the variety of topics discussed in the interview yields some information on this point. In addition to stating what the range of interests seems to be, it should be possible to evaluate their adaptive utility by comparing how adequately he utilizes them in these indirect ways with his over-all efficiency as measured by intelligence tests.

Lastly, it is of crucial importance always to make some judgment, however tentative, about the patient's intellectual ties to reality. One of the frequent problems which the psychologist is asked to help solve is that of borderline conditions involving possible psychosis. Adequacy of reality testing is determined by consensual validation. A patient who says that a table is a table and a chair is a chair is considered to have adequate ties to reality. By the same token, a patient who answers questions on the WAIS appropriately, sees the animals on card VIII of the Rorschach, specifies the sex and age of the TAT figures the way others do, and completes sentences in appropriate fashion is likely to have adequate ties to reality. If the patient can do some of these things but fails in others, it is a question of determining those life situations in which his reality ties fail as opposed to those in which they are adequately retained.

Affective Aspects of Personality

As in previous sections, the trainee is again asked to list hypotheses leading to the prediction of observable behavior.

The ways and means that the patient has developed for dealing with his drives and motives is determined not so much by the content of the projective tests as by the uniqueness of his behavior and its constancy in various situations. From the TAT it may be possible to hypothesize that the patient is very empathetic and easily becomes involved or, conversely, that he is much inclined to shy away from involvement. This instrument should furnish clues to the patient's reaction to people of either sex, peers, subordinates, superordinate figures, etc. The success or failure of the story characters in carrying out their stated objectives may furnish clues as to the patient's own perceived feeling of adequacy or inadequacy. Successful Rorschach predictions have been made concerning a great many ways of dealing with affect. These include a mature blending of affective involvement and rational control, a forced blending of these two, a stereotyped way of dealing with situations of this kind, a brittle, rational control from which affect is excluded, and a complete wallowing in affect devoid of any rational control. Even nonprojective instruments yield valuable clues in this area, for instance a patient's response to the WAIS Similarities item "How are an orange and a banana alike," that "I enjoy eating them both so much" has considerable significance beyond the score itself inasmuch as it reflects his narcissism and his eagerness to enjoy oral pleasures. In this category no attempt is made to specify the content of the patient's drives, but only his methods of dealing with them, whatever they may be.

An attempt is also made under this heading to describe the characteristic mood of the individual. Behavior during the test and the stimulatability of the individual by the various properties of the ink blots furnish pertinent information, but the various thematic tests probably supply the clearest and most directly valuable clues. Having estimated the patient's characteristic mood, there remains the problem of gauging its stability, both within a given test and between tests. As before, knowledge of the unique stimulus properties of each contributing instrument enhances our ability to make differential interpretations.

The examiner assumes that the same basic needs exist in everyone, e.g., passive, aggressive, sexual, dependent, or independent. One individual is distinguished from another not in terms of whether he possesses these needs, but rather in terms of how he responds to them and how they influence his social relationships. In estimating the influence of an individual's behavior upon others it is important to note whether his needs are expressed in an obnoxious, seductive, or fairly smooth fashion. Aggressiveness, for instance, may have constructive or destructive effects. Thus, being intellectually critical of percepts on the Rorschach may be effective or not, depending upon the resultant increase or decrease in form accuracy. Similarly, aggression displayed in stories on the TAT results in either the constructive solution of the posed dilemma or in a helpless floundering around. Sexual needs are frequently mentioned in the psychological reports, but often very little indication is given as to their actual effect upon behavior. Unquestionably, sexual preoccupations infered from symbolic projective material are much more difficult to evaluate in terms of their effect upon

conscious thinking and behavior than are manifest sexual preoccupations, yet sometimes this distinction is not made clear.
It is helpful to the student to confine this category to estimates
of how the patient will actually behave, leaving all theorizing
about underlying causes until the next category.

Basic Conflict Areas

In this box are listed those hypotheses having to do with
etiologic, underlying, or genetic factors. Here the psychologist
is free to make the usual speculations. The hypotheses in this
category need have no necessary behavioral analog. If the conflict is thought to be between two opposing and inconsistent
drives (e.g., dependence versus independence, homosexuality
versus heterosexuality, passivity versus aggressiveness) the inference may be drawn either from a single test or from a combination of tests. For example, the characters in the TAT stories
may be consistently very active, aggressive, masculine individuals who behave in a very dominating manner with little consideration for others. On the other hand, the content and color
dynamics of the Rorschach protocol may symbolize marked
passivity and dependence. Rather than interpret each of these
two sources separately, it is much more useful to combine
them and describe the patients intense dependence-independence
conflict.

Not only may there be a conflict between two inconsistent
drives but also between the expression or inhibition of a single
drive. In such a case the desire to express aggressiveness may
be in opposition to the desire to please other people by inhibiting
it. The basic aggressiveness may manifest itself in the nature of
the lines drawn on the Bender-Gestalt and DAP or in the number and quality of animal movement responses on the Rorschach,
but as the patient is confronted by instruments which permit
the exercise of greater conscious control (Sentence-Completion
Test, MMPI), he may reveal the conciliatory and affiliative
sides of his nature.

The hypotheses falling within this category, while vitally
important, have perhaps been over-emphasized by psychologists
because of their enthusiasm for dynamic theories of personality.
In many clinical settings, however, the hypotheses listed under

other categories may be of more immediate relevance to those who rely upon the psychological report. In any event, the psychologist must be most cautious about not confusing hypotheses of the kind described in this category with those which would lead to direct predictions of conscious self-concept and public behavior.

Adaptive and Maladaptive Techniques

The assumption here is that most psychological traumata involve a loss of self-esteem which in turn produces anxiety. It is supposed that most of the patient's adaptive and maladaptive maneuvers exist to reduce anxiety and re-establish a balanced or homeostatic condition once again, enhancing self-esteem. Included among these are the following:

Compulsion. With the permeation of ego-psychology into everyday psychological language, the concept of compulsion has become relatively familiar and easy to apply in various psychological test situations. For instance, compulsity in the Rorschach is expressed by an overconcern with seeing wholes, by a preoccupation with accuracy, and by the dissection of what is already small into still smaller segments. This technique is seen in the Bender-Gestalt when the patient takes considerable time in order to be accurate, numbers the individual figures, and counts every dot and loop. On the TAT it may take the form of consistent substitution of description for thematization, as well as involvement in all sorts of trivial and inconsequential details. A summary inspection of this horizontal category may reveal that some of these techniques are used consistently throughout, whereas others only come up on certain occasions.

Projection. Projection may be a difficult technique to recognize since to some extent it is called for by the very nature of many of the tests utilized. Yet, its excessive utilization by the patient is frequently evident in the marked idiosyncracy of his reaction. When an inkblot is described with great fervor as being ugly or beautiful, dangerous or seductive, this technique is obviously at work. When TAT or Sentence-Completion protocols take on the flavor of free associations, one becomes aware of the extent to which any stimulus tends to set off the patient's own feelings, without his awareness that this is taking place. Excessive suspicion and demands for further structure always imply that the insecurity is perceived as being part of the environment, since this viewpoint is more ego-syntonic and comforting than perceiving the self as insecure.

Withdrawal. Blocking may take place in response to any one of the stimuli involved in a psychological test battery. Here it becomes important to know not only what test precipitated or exacerbated the withdrawal maneuver, but what part of the test. Certain cards on the Rorschach or TAT, particular Sentence-Completion items, or other specific stimulus situations, may be identified as the basic cause of the withdrawal. The frequency of withdrawal may furnish a clue as to how general such behavior is in everyday situations.

Escape into Fantasy. Except in those instances of manifest psychosis, escape into fantasy is an adaptive technique which can only be determined by looking horizontally across the row at all the tests. Such an escape technique is very difficult under conditions of maximal structure, but becomes increasingly easy and is even passively encouraged by the less structured tests which permit the patient to drift away from the stimulus and into a pleasant world of make-believe. This escape trend is especially apparent when the Rorschach inquiry produces further associations, when one TAT story is merely a take-off point for others, and when the general affect during projective testing is much more favorable than when reality is dragged into the picture by more structured tests or interviews.

These few illustrations provide some idea of how adaptive and maladaptive techniques are gauged from psychological tests. A list of such techniques is virtually inexhaustible, containing such varied methods as conversion, compartmentalization, negativism, humor, isolation, overdependency, and acting out. In each instance the adaptiveness or maladaptiveness must be evaluated not only in terms of the fact or even the degree of its presence or absence, but according to its utility in helping the patient to adjust in terms of the total economy of the organism. Rather than simply reporting "The patient is often quite compulsive," it is more useful to show how the compulsivity is used: "The patient often makes feeble attempts at using compulsive techniques which are not at all effectual either in improving the efficiency of his performance or in reducing the severe anxiety from which he suffers," is different than "The patient's anxiety is well-bound by consistent and effective compulsive techniques that are manifest throughout and permit him to be much more efficient in many life situations than would otherwise be possible." Similarly, it is not enough to say merely that the patient tends to project. The test finding has more meaning when put into a context: "The patient's tendency to project himself into many situations creates a kind of flexibility in his interpersonal behavior which reduces friction. This unwillingness to face the basic nature of his drives blinds him to many of his motives, but this fact does not seem to be any particular problem to him" or "The patient's chronic tendency to attribute his own feelings to everyone about him produces a complete lack of ability on his part to react appropriately to friendly overtures from others and creates a constant state of mutual antagonism."

Diagnostic Aspects

This category contains hypotheses which may have some ultimate bearing upon the diagnosis of the patient. Inserting such an hypothesis in a given box within this category does not necessarily mean that it will find its way into the final report, but instead signifies that within this specific test modality the patient behaved in a manner suggesting the possibility of a particular kind of pathology. Trainees will soon learn the process of rationalizing results to fit an early hypothesis. Before they go too far in this direction emphasis in supervision should be placed upon the necessity for evaluating each instrument in terms of its own contribution to the understanding of the patient, whether or not each aspect will be part of the final conclusion.

The statements in this category should not be test "signs" or "indicators" but second-order inferences pertaining to disturbances in thinking or behavior thought to characterize various pathologic syndromes. Much of the data to be specified here are really duplications of points made in earlier sections of the outline, including intellectual and affective aspects, as well as adaptive and maladaptive techniques. Replication at this point prepares ultimately for a diagnostic summary based upon the outline, frequently one of the main objectives of the psychological report.

In terms of feeling free to make diagnostic hypotheses, it should be kept in mind that some tests have been exposed to considerably more research in this area than others. The fact that the Rorschach and the MMPI can therefore probably be most safely used for this particular purpose should not prevent a psychologist from noting disorganized thinking, disorientation, confusion, inadequate regulation of the environment, and similar schizophrenic-like thinking characteristics on tests like the TAT, CAT, and MAPS. Similarly, the patient's behavior both between and during tests can verify such tendencies as overdependency and somatization that tend to characterize neurotic conditions. The psychologist frequently ends up with the suggestion of a personality disorder by eliminating many of these symptoms. When both neurotic and psychotic manifestations are conspicious by their absence, it is often possible to speculate that both the basic conflicts noted and the adaptive techniques employed are more built-in and characterologic than transient and symptomatic. In any case, the final diagnosis suggested by the psychological examiner should be based upon an integration of the statements listed under each column heading.

Prognostic Implications

In this box the trainee is required to list separately under each test the implications for the future adjustment of the patient, either with or without reference to the possible efficacy of various treatment procedures. This final step in completing the outline form should take into account the vast predictive literature available. If electric shock therapy is being considered, the special scales and predictive measures developed in connection with it should be considered. Similarly, if tranquillization is in question, the likelihood of a resultant modification in behavior could be gauged.

Probably the most specific comments can be made when psychotherapy is proposed. The various projective instruments may lead to the prediction of distinctive reactions to different therapists. There are TAT and Rorschach cards as well as specific items in the Sentence-Completion Test which are either designed or have been empirically found to stimulate the patient's characteristic reactions to authority or authoritative persons. Both the phenomenology of the patient's reactions to projective tests and the content of many of his responses provide clues for predicting how dependency will manifest itself in a psychotherapeutic situation. For example, a person's TAT stories might demonstrate a consistent theme of passing responsibility on to someone else, which in turn may be reacted to either by a comfortable giving in or by a sort of "dog in the manger" attitude toward the necessity of giving up independence. On another level, the content of his Rorschach responses may indicate an underlying passive proclivity or a basic struggle for independence which is being consistently frustrated by fear of failure.

Again, tests such as the TAT, Picture Frustration, and Sentence-Completion may provide specific information as to the specific life situations most likely to arouse anxiety and constitute stress for the individual. Information of this kind may save the therapist much time in deciding where to focus and how far to go in making interpretations.

Perhaps most important is an evaluation of over-all ego strength and the degree of subjective discomfort of which the patient is capable. Many clues are manifested in the various psychological test situations regarding the patient's desire for change and the degree of change that he can tolerate without undue anxiety. In the case of specific problems, such as marital difficulties, the psychologist may wish to draw specific inferences about the patient's capability for meeting the needs of another person concerning whom an equal amount of information is available.

SUPERVISION

Column Approach

The supervisor refers to the first column of the outline to determine the test administered. He then reviews the test, makes his own interpretations, and examines the student's interpretations as organized in this first column. If the student has made some interpretations which are not clear to the supervisor, he is asked to explain and document them. If necessary, pertinent literature and basic textbook material is reviewed and a subsequent discussion between student and supervisor often results in both of them learning more and one of them altering his opinion. If the supervisor makes certain interpretations which have not occurred to the student, a similar working-out process occurs. At the end of this discussion, each column should represent the joint effort of both parties. This same procedure is followed for each succeeding column, making it necessary for the student to bring to bear all of his resources for the interpretation of each of the instruments employed. Consequently, he is not able to get by with merely recording an IQ or some single intellectual function as a way of summarizing the intelligence test data. All the various implications concerning personality that he has gauged from this test are brought into the open and subjected to discussion with the supervisor. It is quite legitimate to draw an inference from a single test which will not appear in the final report.

Row Approach

In the second part of the supervision the focus is on the rows rather than the columns. The behavior of the individual is discussed in terms of its variation from one stimulus situation to the next. Seemingly incongruent interpretations under "Intellectual aspects," for example, are examined in this part of the supervisory session, with the patient perhaps appearing much more intellectually efficient on one test than on another. Although superficially these interpretations may appear inconsistent, they are in reality all part of the same pattern and should be brought into harmony before being communicated to the referent. Similarly, under "Affective aspects of the personality," the patient may appear much more withdrawn under one set of circumstances than under another, or he may show different kinds and degrees of control in one test situation as distinct from others. Patients suffering from thought disturbances very frequently demonstrate a much greater degree of pathology in the Rorschach test than in the Bender-Gestalt, while those suffering from organic brain damage tend to show much *less* pathology on the Rorschach. On the other hand, one who shows a complete lack of empathetic ability on the TAT may reveal positive potential in this area on the Rorschach, lending more depth and breadth to the final interpretation.

The test-taking attitude demonstrated by the "validity" scales of the MMPI may well enable the psychologist to place some of the other test data into a more comprehensible frame of reference. Thus, an individual attempting to present a better picture of himself, as compared to one who appears quite confused, may behave in ways that are superficially similar but subject to basically different interpretations. This approach makes it much more difficult for the trainee to ignore pertinent but seemingly incongruous elements of his total test battery than is usually the case. If, as happens upon occasion, it seems impossible to rationalize these disparate behaviors, this fact should also be made clear in the final report. If the basic assumption that behavior is always determined and basically consistent is accepted, failure to bring harmony to the pattern is seen more as an outcome of our current state of ignorance and ineffectuality in dealing with such complex matters than as the result of any inherent inadequacy of the test instruments themselves.

REPORT WRITING

The trainee is next instructed to write the report, putting aside all of the raw data and using only the amended outline.

The plan of the outline fits in very well with most of the organizing principles set forth in the preceding chapter. The first row can be used as the basis of a series of behavioral observations, while the next four rows serve as a section on data analysis, and the last two can be integrated into a final section embodying the conclusions and recommendations. Since the tests themselves will already have been thoroughly discussed and ample supervision given in this area, the focus here is solely on communication.

This procedure is considered more adequate for supervision

and communication than the test-oriented report. The kind of supervision thus afforded the trainee should make for better psychological reports with tighter organization and, incidentally, better trained clinical psychologists. By this method the report can be tailored very specifically to fit the needs of the referents, both primary and secondary, thereby conforming to the requirements set forth by Hammond and Allen (12).

6
LANGUAGE OF THE REPORT

PSYCHOLOGICAL reports must be written in understandable English to communicate. As part of their striving for invulnerability, psychologists often resort to professional jargon which may be meaningful to them but is of little value to anyone else. It is almost as though they were subscribing to the dictum "If you cannot clarify, mystify."

What is to be considered technical language in any given instance depends very much upon who the primary and secondary readers may be. Even common psychiatric terms may not always be appropriate. The incomprehensible complexity may not lie in the word itself, but may be implicit in the concept being utilized. Psychologists often implicitly assume an understanding of psychoanalytic or other theory-related concepts on the part of the reader which may be totally unjustified. They may, for example, assume that the reader is fully aware of the connection between repressed hostility and guilt, the effect of oedipal conflict upon attitudes towards women, the results of sibling rank, or the theory that various symptoms serve as a defense against anxiety and contribute to a restoration of self-esteem.

Foster states explicitly his opposition to "shop talk," by which he means the ultratechnical language of the psychologist who uses test categories as a means of communication. Palmer agrees very strongly with this point of view. Holzberg et al. question whether the use of technical language really fosters recognition of the psychologist as a scientifically trained person. They feel that this can only be demonstrated by presentation by the psychologist of logical and convincing evidence in support of his interpretations and generalizations. They argue that "the injudicious and unexplained use of such terms as 'extratensive,' 'flexor,' 'deterioration,' 'succorance need,' etc., while ringing with scientific erudition, will only result in isolating the psychologist from his professional colleagues."

The most thoroughgoing study of language as it is used in psychological reports is probably that of Grayson and Tolman (11). These authors culled 28 psychological reports from which they selected 50 crucial terms, each presented within an illustrative context. The judges in the study, whose task it was to define these terms in their own words, consisted of 20 psychologists and 17 psychiatrists. Among their more important findings were the following:

1.   Psychologists were generally wordier than the psychiatrists in the definitions that they proposed, perhaps owing to a temperamental characteristic of the psychologist which makes him somewhat intellectually pretentious and verbose. Perhaps the length of time spent by the psychologist during his training in an academic setting causes his explanations to take on a rather pedantic flavor and produce the impression of the eternal instructor, even in this context.

2.   Psychologists generally were more intellectual and circuitous.

3.   There were distinct and significant differences between psychologists and psychiatrists in the meanings they attributed to the 50 common terms.

4.   There were many individual differences within both groups, although these were greater among the psychiatrists. This result suggests that although the psychologists tend to be somewhat idiosyncratic as a group, they tend to be consistently and reliably so as opposed to the psychiatrists.

5.   Many of the terms were defined vaguely and loosely by both groups of judges.

The reader would profit from a careful study of this paper. The terms studied are very common and appear every day in psychological reports. The wide differences in conception on the part of some psychologists and psychiatrists is noteworthy. "Aggression" was variously defined as positive assertion and hostile acting out. "Anxiety," interestingly enough, was defined more physiologically by the group of psychologists and more dynamically by the psychiatrists. "Bizarre" was used in the sense of mild deviation by the psychiatrists and as signifying a pathological extreme by the psychologists. The attempt on the part of the psychologist to appear scientific was demonstrated by his tendency to bend over backwards in giving biological and chemical analogs as often as possible. The group of psychiatrists used in the study tended perhaps to be overly biased in a psychoanalytic direction, although many of their definitions were more in accord with lay usage than were those of the psychologists.

Another related study is an unpublished one by Suczek and myself. A number of similar terms were arranged in a check-list. Under each item several subcategories were suggested. The instructions were to appropriately classify the patient according to the psychiatric findings. This check-list was given to psychiatrists, clinical psychologists, psychiatric social workers, and advanced trainees in these fields, following a staff conference which included an interview with the patient by the psychiatric consultant, presentation of the social history by the worker, the clinical history by the psychiatric resident, and presentation of the psychological findings by the clinical psychology trainee. Agreement among the group on the check-list was found to be virtually restricted to those personality characteristics which had been the subject of specific discussion by the consultant and on which he had made a definite pronouncement. Otherwise, the agreement was not beyond chance expectancy. It seems possible that some of this unreliability resulted from the kind of semantic difficulty brought out in the study by Grayson and Tolman.

Test Jargon

Every test has its own jargon. Associated with the Rorschach are $W\%$, number of M, P, *impotence*, *perplexity*, *contamination*, *confabulation*, etc. Some of these are readily recognized as technical Rorschach terms. Those less readily recognized as referring exclusively to this particular test present, perhaps, the greater danger, since they have other meanings in general psychiatry or in common everyday language. The Szondi utilizes another set of mysterious letters with their own particular meanings. An increasing problem with the introduction of more and more projective tests is that a given symbol may refer to more than one test: K on the Szondi, with its implication of narcissism and possible withdrawal from the world of living objects, may be confused with *K* on the MMPI and its reference to a test-taking attitude characterized by the appearance of adequate or exaggerated ego-defenses. Another kind of hazard is illustrated by the psychological report writer who, in reference to the fact that hands were seen in pockets on the DAP, assumes that the reader will share his faith in the inevitable presence of guilt feelings concerning masturbation hypothesized by Machover. Again, psychologists employing the TAT may slip into a discussion of various *needs* and *presses* a la Murray.

Use of such test-oriented terminology places the clinical psychologist in double jeopardy. First, he will not be understood by many of the people reading his report. Whether the report is used in other agencies or by psychologists employing a different system of appraisal or scoring, or whether it be used by a consultant who is hopeful that it will help to unravel the complexities of the case confronting him, frustration and misunderstanding will be the inevitable result. The other horn of the dilemma is that this kind of language will inevitably result in poor organization and an unreadable style.

The psychological test should not be a shibboleth to be refuted or defended at any cost. Each diagnostic tool is a means to an end rather than an end in itself. From this point of view, the psychologist will very shortly come to think in behavioral terms as he interprets a test rather than restrict his interest to ways of classifying or ordering its data.

One reason that has been offered for using test-oriented language is that it is necessary in order to do an adequate job of supervising the trainee. Yet, if the supervisory method described in the previous chapter is employed, this need will be greatly diminished. Consequently, it seems difficult to justify the use of this kind of language. It hampers communication and has other obvious disadvantages.

Technical Psychological and Psychiatric Terms

The Grayson and Tolman study has demonstrated quite thoroughly that the assumption of ready and easy communication between psychologists and psychiatrists through the medium of certain common terms is a rather doubtful one. The academic and clinical background of these two professions does seem to make a difference. Also, perhaps the psychologist, being still relatively new in the situation, has psychological needs which are met by being intellectually esoteric. On the other hand, it seems unreasonable to expose the lay reader to terms like "chronic ambulatory schizophrenia," "stimulus-response patterns," "hysteroid personality," "the technique of compartmentalization," or "emotional lability." At perhaps a slightly different level of discourse are some terms which could probably be understood within the joint fields of psychology and education, such as "sibling," "intellectual potential," "educable" or "trainable," but ask the man in the street the meaning of these terms and he will be quite puzzled, despite their apparent simplicity.

The use of such technical terms is certainly justified under some circumstances. If the psychologist is working in a psychiatric setting where all of the members of the staff are fully trained people, he is freer to use psychiatric terms without fear of rebuff, but he must first make sure that the terms found in the test manuals are being used in the report to the psychiatrists according to the latter's frame of reference and not some other. Certainly "confabulation" as used in psychiatry does not mean the same thing as when the clinical psychologist uses the term in reference to the Rorschach. English and English (6) define confabulation as (1) unsystematic falsification of memory and (2) (Rorschach) a category for unorganized and rambling inkblot responses. (If the authors had been more accurate on the second count their definition would have described a response in which a small detail is perceived accurately but with inappropriate generalization to the total situation.) To assume that these meanings are basically the same is rather gratuitous indeed. If the psychologist is writing a report for someone in a medical setting where the assumption of psychiatric training cannot be made legitimately, he might still feel free to use strictly medical terms. Bear in mind, however, that many physicians who have been working in psychiatric institutions for many years lack the theoretical training or interest required to acquaint them with some of the psychoanalytic terms that clinical psychologists so frequently choose to employ. In an educational setting the use of terms comprehensive to the educator certainly would be appropriate. Where psychologists are merely attempting to communicate with one another, any sort of language would presumably do for communication (or competition), so long as it really *did* serve to communicate.

Basic English

It is my contention that any statement found in psychological reports could be made comprehensible to any literate individual of at least average intelligence. For example, the idea that an individual possesses "empathy" could be stated as follows: "The patient can understand and sympathize with the feelings of others, since he finds it relatively easy to put himself in their place." In reference to "impotence" it might be pointed out that "This individual has a constant feeling of inadequacy in dealing with some of the complex situations of everyday life. He feels powerless when faced with situations seemingly requiring strength and effort." "Hostility towards the father figure" might be translated "The patient is so fearful and suspicious of people in positions of authority that he automatically assumes an aggressive attitude towards them, being sure that swift retaliation will follow. He doesn't give such people an opportunity to demonstrate their real characteristics since he assumes that they are all alike." Instead of describing the patient as having "level of aspiration difficulties" the statement could read: "The patient is not satisfied with his role in life, but feels himself cut out for bigger and better things which he accomplishes in imagination rather than actually striving to achieve."

If the clinical psychologist himself really comprehends what he is attempting to communicate, a technical language level is really unnecessary. Abstract terms are a shorthand method of communication and are useful for this purpose if addressed to the proper person. If not addressed to the particular audience of the report, they may become insurmountable barriers to communication and consequently be open to vigorous attack.

In a study of the Szondi Test I completed some years ago (15), it was necessary to draw up descriptions of various psychiatric categories which would be easily comprehensible to the lay reader. These included the usual categories of homosexuality, sadism, epilepsy, etc., associated with this test. The problems encountered in arriving at these descriptions were manifold. Apparently clinical psychologists feel quite comfortable talking about syndromes in their own private jargon, but find it difficult to really couch an explanation in general operational terms.

I have presented the results of psychological tests to a variety of audiences, including groups of people in related professions as well as those at subprofessional and nonprofessional levels. It has been possible in almost every such instance to clarify the nature of the contribution made by the psychological battery to the satisfaction of the audience. For instance, it was possible to convey to a group of occupational therapy aides what the results of psychological tests may signify in the choice of activities, and the meaning to the patient of those activities in the occupational therapy setting.

Discussion with nurses and psychiatric aides concerning the behavioral and therapeutic implications of the psychological tests for their work has involved citing actual illustrative material and clarifying the phenomenology, logical background, and behavioral analog of this material in respect to the setting in which they were operating. This procedure can only be followed if the psychologist is able not only to translate the results of his tests into basic English, but is actually able to think in these terms. When concepts become tools rather than ritualistic terms which serve to reduce the psychologist's anxiety resulting from his feelings of insecurity, he is more willing to give them up or modify them. (Parenthetically, students are much more inclined to read current psychological literature when it is written simply than when it is written in professional jargon.)

Here are some further examples of translating technical concepts into basic English:

1. "The patient projects extensively" becomes "The patient has a tendency to attribute to other people feelings and ideas originating within himself regardless of how these other people might feel."

2. "The patient is extremely narcissistic" becomes "The

patient is so intensely preoccupied with himself that he finds it very difficult to become interested in other people."

3. "The patient is extremely defensive" becomes "The patient tries to avoid recognition of his own feelings, since they threaten his security by making him appear irrational and unstable."

4. "The defenses the patient uses are . . ." becomes "The methods characteristically employed by the patient for reducing anxiety are . . ."

5. "Latent homosexuality is quite a problem to the patient" becomes "Much of the patient's present discomfort can be attributed to unrecognized feelings of sexual attraction to other men which make him tense in their presence and which tend to alienate him from women."

6. "The patient's interests appear rather stereotyped" becomes "The patient is currently preoccupied with certain matters to the exclusion of others. If this state of affairs is permanent it may make it difficult for him to extend his horizons."

7. "The patient has level of aspiration difficulties" becomes "The patient prefers to imagine himself performing deeds in fantasy, but has difficulty focusing upon the current everyday struggle for existence and being satisfied with what he can actually achieve."

8. "The patient's reaction to mother figures is generally negative" becomes "The thought of older women seems rather unpleasant to the patient."

9. "The patient's attitude towards his wife is extremely ambivalent" becomes "The patient is greatly attracted to his wife and has many positive feelings towards her, although at the same time he can be intensely irritated by her and feel quite antagonistic."

10. "The patient suffers from free-floating anxiety" becomes "The patient often feels very uncomfortable and ill at ease without really recognizing the reason for this feeling or being able to do anything about it."

11. "The patient's hostility seems very much repressed" becomes "Whatever hostility the patient may experience has

been excluded from awareness because of the discomfort it arouses."

12. "The patient's seductive manner has been constantly reinforced" becomes "Because when this patient behaved seductively she has usually got her way, she was encouraged to continue this form of behavior."

13. "The dynamics of the personality are . . . " becomes "Some of the interesting characteristics of this individual seem to be . . . "

14. "The motivational system seems to be . . . " becomes "Some of the underlying causes of the patient's behavior are . . . "

15. "This patient has a great need for affiliation" becomes "This patient would very much like to have friends."

Summary

An attempt has been made to illustrate some of the language problems which characterize the communication of psychological findings. Only one study has really investigated this area to any degree. It is hoped that others will follow. However, it is abundantly clear even now that many assumptions are being made about the communication value of technical terms which would not bear close scrutiny. Three kinds of language often used in psychological reports have been discussed and a bias in favor of greater simplicity expressed.

Experience in supervision seems to dictate that a greater sophistication and understanding of psychological tests on the part of the student is required for communication in basic English than is required for communication at any other level. The more thorough kind of thinking-through necessitated by this form of writing will inevitably lead to better communication and consequently better service. Individuals are encouraged to develop thier own communicative resources.

7

RELATIONSHIP OF THE REPORT TO OTHER SOURCES OF INFORMATION

Information Available Prior to Psychological Evaluation

ONE COMMON question is whether psychological evaluations are more "objective" when carried on without other knowledge or information about the patient. One extreme viewpoint insists that psychological test data are like other laboratory findings and are therefore best discovered in a sterile atmosphere devoid of all contaminating phenomena. The assumption is that both the examiner and the test situation can be ruled out as variables markedly affecting the examination; however, recent studies have failed to bear out this assumption, indicating instead the very real influence of these variables.

Another extreme viewpoint is the "subjective" position of some authors who use the psychological test stimuli as the basis of an extensive series of free associations. Questioning the accuracy of their statements or "interpretations" brings forth charges of being excessively cold and scientific (the two terms being considered synonymous).

Some middle ground between these two extremes should be possible. To evaluate psychological data and write reports independent of other knowledge about the patient is useful from a training standpoint, and may be defensible from a research standpoint, but is difficult to defend from a purely clinical standpoint. When people's lives and futures are at stake, when important decisions concerning their welfare are to be made, every possible source of information should be exploited. It goes without saying that not only do psychological tests take on added significance when viewed in the light of other available information, but the latter is enhanced by the contributions of the psychological tests. Consequently, there is good and sufficient reason why a well-staffed agency makes its decisions on the basis of a team approach in which information from various sources is pooled for the benefit of the patient and the welfare of society. Any other procedure when important decisions are to be made seems not only unsound but ethically questionable.

In line with the approach of ego-psychology, it is important to know something about the individual's life history so that some idea can be obtained of his resources and adaptive techniques and how successful they have been. Temperament, sociability, tolerance for ambiguity, and ability to withstand stress differs from subject to subject and can be determined partially by studying the adaptive techniques he has used in various life situations. Certain objective clues to the patient's efficiency come from his past vocational and avocational successes and failures. Statements about him by others may not provide objective information, but they do reveal the nature of his interpersonal techniques and the success of the ego in organizing and regulating the interpersonal environment to meet his basic needs.

To aid in assessing the validity of inferences drawn from psychological tests, it is certainly important to have as many collateral sources of information as possible. According to Sargent's (20) scheme of overlapping pyramids, the same inferential structure can be created from the observations of social workers, nurses, and others, as from psychological tests. At the very least, the psychologist should thoroughly review the patient's chart and question all of those in the clinic or hospital who have been able to observe him. Better still, records of his past achievements and failures should be studied, as well as the reports from all those in his family circle who can possibly be interviewed.

Levels of Inference within the Psychological Evaluation

Before comparing psychological test data with other sources of information, it is necessary to determine the nature of the process whereby responses to inkblots, the creation of stories around pictures, the reproduction of geometrical designs, and other simple tasks, lead to such complex and seemingly remote predictions by the psychologist. The inferential scheme implicit in the proposed organization of the psychological report is in essence identical with that proposed by Sargent. The raw data which she puts at the baseline are the actual facts of both test response and behavior during testing and are, presumably, more reliably obtainable and the result of direct observation rather than inference. However, Sargent seems to detract from the purity of her scheme by utilizing test scores at this baseline level, with perhaps insufficient recognition that such scores are sometimes quite unreliable and entail certain inferences (as in the case of the Rorschach). These baseline observations are assumed to be congruent with data collected by the nurse, factual material related to the social worker by relatives of the patient, and verbatim statements made by the patient to the psychiatrist.

The next level of inference (Sargent's first inference level) consists of a slightly higher order of data-sorting. Here information from different media is collated and an attempt is made to describe behavior which, because of its multidimensional source, may be thought to have more general predictive efficiency. It is sometimes doubtful, however, whether behavior that is regarded as analogous from one test to the next is actually so, since so much research remains to be done in this area. Neither of these two levels are explicit in the psychological report. This part of the clinical psychologist's work, like the raw notes of the investigator, finds its way into the wastebasket and is often lost to further scrutiny. Part of the inferential process at this level could well consist of attempting to test reality by observing the patient in standard stimulus situations of *different* kinds, being alert for seeming incongruities, and postponing the process of rationalization long enough to learn the lesson that although behavior is presumed to be consistent, this consistency is sometimes difficult to recognize.

With the third procedural step (Sargent's second inferential level), the preferred personality theory of the psychologist begins to find application. At this point, the ego psychologist will begin to talk about adaptive and maladaptive devices, the orthodox analyst about oedipal conflicts and castration fears, the learning theorist about positive and negative feedback and reinforcement. It is crucial in making inferences at this level to distinguish between perceived pressures upon the individual

and perceived stimuli that originate within him. Prior to form-
ing an abstraction which usually takes the place of a nosological
classification (Sargent's apex), it is also vital to distinguish
latent from manifest pathology. The scheme thought most useful for this purpose is that of Leary (16) who has described five
levels of the personality, three of which are relevent here:

Level of Public Communication. This level refers to direct perceptions of the individual by others. It consists essentially of a
description of his social stimulus-value as perceived by his peers,
subordinates, superordinates, same sex and opposite-sex figures,
enemies, and friends. All of these are asked to evaluate the
individual's traits and characteristics, assets and liabilities,
and their evaluations are pooled in some way. When these data
are referred to in the psychological report, it should be possible
to include a statement that clearly predicts observable behavior
which can be consensually validated to some extent by the
reader if he has the opportunity to observe the patient directly.
However, it behooves the psychologist to be most circumspect
and cautious in making these predictions from many of the tests
he employs. Is he certain that behavior in intelligence tests will
be equivalent to behavior in the work situation? Is enough
known about the phenomenology of the Rorschach test to
predict with accuracy the approach to other life situations?
Is enough known about the relationship between fantasy and
behavior to hazard any guesses concerning overt behavior from
fantasy materials on thematic tests? It is characteristic of both
clinical psychologists and psychiatrists that they rarely investigate overt behavior directly, but instead attempt to predict it
from measures which are really more appropriate to other
levels. It is the psychiatric social worker who ordinarily focuses
her investigative methods directly on a patient's social stimulus-
value, making a very vital contribution to the multilevel assessment of the individual. Since a social history is ordinarily
available in the adequately staffed agency, psychologists are
wise to restrain themselves from making unnecessarily hazardous
predictions at this level.

Level of Conscious Perception. This level, described by Leary,
refers to those self-perceptions of the individual which he is
willing to communicate to others. It is supposed that many
of our psychological tests measure this level directly. At one
time or another this assumption has been made concerning the

MMPI, the Sentence-Completion test, and even the Thematic Apperception Test. Some current research of mine casts considerable doubt on these assumptions. The interview is also generally considered to focus explicitly on this level, despite the fact that other levels may also be involved. It seems very difficult for clinical psychologists in their reports to speak directly of the patient's conscious self-concept. They insist on reading between the lines rather than taking the patient's word for anything he says. The end result is an unfortunate muddling of communication. If the psychological report were to contain explicit statements as to (a) what the patient thinks about himself, and (b) what the psychologist perceives the patient to be thinking about himself, it might be helpful. The assumption that the patient's explicit statements of self-evaluation are completely valueless appears rather gratuitous.

Level of Private Symbolization. This level Leary rather diffusely defines as the level measured by projective instruments. His choice of the term "preconscious" is rather unfortunate in view of its previous connotations in the psychoanalytic literature. Leary certainly does not assume that all projective material is at the same level. There is an implicit thread throughout his discussion which seems to presuppose that eventually projective material will be sorted along a hierarchy according to its distance from the level of conscious communication. The development of such a hierarchy is a crucial research problem in the area of personality assessment, one in which many people are currently working.

Much of the material contained in psychological reports is presumed to be at this level of personality—both nonconscious and nonpublic, yet somehow motivating and influencing the individual's life. In the communication of such material, it is crucial that the psychologist be constantly aware that he is speaking at a nonbehavioral level. Clinical psychologists who have not been made aware of this problem in communication often speak of these private level phenomena as though they were either predicting behavior directly or else discussing the conscious content of the patient's thinking. This theoretical carelessness is probably influential in confusing (and alienating) members of other professions who cannot be expected to be clearer about what is being communicated than is the psychologist himself.

It is therefore suggested that *accurate specification of level* is an indispensable feature of the psychological report. The psychologist in his role as a consultant can legitimately make inferences about the patient and his behavior as a whole and can make recommendations as to his re-education or treatment, but he should take these steps on the basis of more information than just the results of the psychological evaluation.

Relating Psychological and other Information Following Submission of the Report

Unfortunately, many professional and subprofessional workers in the mental hygiene field are unaware of the extent to which the overt behavior they observe may differ from and yet be basically consistent with other levels of the personality. It is possible to sit at many a staff conference and listen to colleagues engage in fruitless debate resulting from inadequate sophistication in this area. A more comprehensive approach is implied in the statement made by the Director of Professional Services in a large Veterans Administration hospital who said, "If the projective tests bring out the same things as the clinical observations, I think that's nice. But when they bring out something different, then that's important." He was saying that personality is such a complex phenomenon to investigate and to comprehend that light from every new angle illuminates new areas and helps to bring the total personality into sharper focus.

At a staff conference a clinical psychology trainee reported that "the IQ was at the mentally defective level." The psychiatric resident vigorously objected, referring to the patient's work history as evidence that he was not mentally defective. He said that the psychologist was wrong and that the IQ was not as claimed. Here there is obviously a lack of understanding concerning the role of the psychological report. The IQ is a test score. If the test in question has been administered and scored in the standardized manner, then there is no doubt about the results. Were the psychologist to go further and suggest that the individual was actually a mental defective on the basis of such flimsy evidence as an intelligence test, then indeed he would be laying himself open to criticism. But when the psychiatric resident criticizes the validity of the "IQ," he is merely revealing his own lack of knowledge concerning the limitations of the test. Actually, both the patient's work history and his intelligence test score are data which must be included, probably together with additional material, in order to have an adequate over-all evaluation of the patient's intellectual resources. No one of these data alone are sufficient for such a purpose.

Our ultimate goal in relating the psychological report to other sources of information is to determine what assets the individual has that will help his eventual adjustment. There are times when psychological test data point to resources which other professional staff members may be unaware of, or to ego weaknesses which should be carefully considered before planning proceeds much further. In the latter instance a distinction must be made between those ego weaknesses which are really strengths because they serve constructive and creative purposes (regression in the service of the ego) and those which actually contribute to interpersonal inefficiency and increasing loss of self-esteem.

Summary

It is important that the psychological report represent the best that the profession can offer. By itself it is only one of many possible approaches to the understanding of the patient. If there is something in the data that exists as a "possibility" a note to this effect should probably be included in the report, but with adequate assurance that it will not be taken as a certainty by the reader. At the same time it is important to keep in mind what the limitations of the referent are for carrying out the recommendations that might be made. The psychological findings should always be integrated with other data before any conclusions are drawn or recommendations made, and the level of the phenomenon being predicted should always be clearly specified. If the psychologist is ever in doubt as to what or what not to include in his psychological report, he should be guided by the basic ethical code of the profession which advocates the welfare of society as the ultimate criterion.

8
BARRIERS TO COMMUNICATION
AND THEIR RESOLUTION

IN THEIR ATTEMPTS to communicate to others and to one another, psychologists find some of their problems to be interpersonal in nature. Sometimes troubled by matters of status and prestige, they are then prone to engage in attempts to maintain their self-esteem. Occasionally their efforts to communicate are hampered by excessive hostility or obsequiousness toward the referent. Much space has been devoted in the literature to so-called interprofessional difficulties, especially between psychologists and psychiatrists, the latter constituting the main body of referents. My feeling is that most of these problems, both "interprofessional" and "intraprofessional," are fundamentally interpersonal. They must be dealt with by the individual psychologist just as he deals with any other motivational conflicts that interfere with his efficiency. It is essential that he gain conscious control over them and not let them continue to influence him to the possible detriment of the patients he is called upon to assist.

One of the barriers to communication frequently reported is a difference in theoretical frame of reference between the psychologist and the referent. It is questionable whether a given psychological report derives from any particular theory because only some of the commonly used psychological instruments are based on a specifically designated theory. For example, the Blacky Pictures are explicitly related to Freud's theory of psychosexual development. The Picture Frustration Test specifically derives from Rosenzweig's own theory of frustration and aggression. The Thematic Apperception Test was presented by Henry Murray in terms of his own modification of Freud's contributions concerning the influences upon the individual of stimuli both from within himself (needs) and from the exter-

nal environment (presses). Rorschach's test was related to some
of the dichotomous conceptualizations of Carl Gustav Jung,
but here the author's own ambivalence towards his mentor
tended to muddy the waters and produce confusion. With
instruments like the Szondi the situation becomes increasingly
complicated. It is debatable whether Susan Deri's (5) attempts
to produce an integration between Freud and Lewin can be
regarded as a theoretical frame of reference. When considering
tests such as the Sentence Completion and the Draw-A-Person
a real never-never land of theorizing appears, in which every
clinician is on his own and is inclined to take advantage of the
carte blanche offered by those distributing the instrument.

In spite of the fact that test batteries as a whole are not
clearly related to any particular theory, some psychologists
insist upon couching their reports in specifically technical terms.
Such terms may result not only in distortion of the intent of the
authors of the various instruments, but makes it difficult to
communicate findings to others. The person reading the report,
whether he is the main referent or somebody else, may be so
puzzled or alienated by the terminology employed and the
theory implied that any further attempts to communicate with
him may prove more difficult. Even when the report writer and
his reader are members of the same school of thought, their
communication may virtually ignore the stimuli and their
predictive capabilities for the sake of using catch words and
favorite symbols. It is suggested that communication is best
carried out by assuming that psychological tests are all standard
methods of observation from which certain specified predictions
can be made. Which predictions can validly and reliably be
made can be determined from the vast literature in the field of
psychological testing, a source not always sufficiently used by
many practicing clinicians. The organization, focus, and style
of the psychological report should all have one objective, and
one objective only—to communicate those findings of which
the clinical psychologist is relatively certain and which will be
of some practical use in formulating further plans for the patient.

Another potential barrier to communication is the pressure
sometimes imposed upon the clinical psychologist to communicate findings about many patients in a relatively brief period,

without allowing him adequate time to thoroughly digest the material. There are those who feel that the main value of psychological tests in the busy clinic or hospital is that they save the psychiatrist time in getting to the bottom of the patient's difficulties and in detecting the basic conflicts that exist, along with the ego resources which may determine the particular treatment. On the other hand, there are those situations which emphasize training and where quality rather than quantity is of prime importance. Such training emphasis makes greater demands upon the psychologist, forcing him to exercise greater discrimination in what he communicates. At the same time, it provides him with sufficient time to digest material thoroughly and bring to bear all the resources he has accumulated through his training, experience, and basic receptivity to the material, encouraging him to produce a result of which he can be proud and which will be maximally useful to others. Whichever system is involved, it is quite essential that all parties involved understand the time factor and that no one feel under such pressure as to make him shoddy or careless in his communicative endeavors.

Another very significant barrier to communication is bias. This matter is illustrated in a neat study by Robinson and Cohen (19) in which they rated the psychological reports of three interns in clinical psychology. A number of statements occuring in these reports were classified and compared from individual to individual. It was found that there were definite and statistically significant differences in statements dealing with aggression-abasement and dependence-independence. The authors raised a number of questions on the basis of this study concerning the use of psychological findings in rating behavior. They suggested that students should be made aware of their biases so as to gain conscious control over them. Another relevant study is one carried on by Garfield, Heine and Leventhal (10), who presented a group of 16 psychological reports to a group of professional judges composed of social workers, psychiatrists, and psychologists. They found that social workers were generally least critical, giving the highest value ratings to the reports, and that the ratings of psychiatrists were generally lower, but more variable than that of psychologists, whose ratings were the most consistent and stable. This seems to indicate that there is a value bias regarding psychological reports which may depend on the relationship of the clinician to the referent.

It is, of course, quite obvious that any maladaptive technique used by a clinical psychologist in attempting to communicate psychological findings will serve as a basis for distortions. A clinical psychologist may easily project his own problems onto many patients that he sees. He may have blind spots which consistently cause him to overlook certain conflicts in other individuals and therefore fail to adequately detect their problems. He may demonstrate reaction formations to certain kinds of drives and, as a result, lean over backwards to present in an excessively benign and glossed-over manner certain difficulties that his clients demonstrate.

Another common kind of bias inherent in psychological reports is what might be called the "maladjustment bias"— the traditional tendency on the part of the clinical psychologist to look for pathology rather than strength. This tendency is partly attributable to his training in a medical setting. Our most modern conception of the purpose of psychological reports includes a focus on strength as well as weakness, on adaptive methods as well as maladaptive ones, and on "signs" of mental health as well as mental illness. That this fact is so often insufficiently emphasized by clinical psychologists may be a reflection of the relative lack of emphasis in their training on *global* personality assessment. On the other hand it may be a function of the pressure imposed in the psychiatric setting to contribute information leading to nosologic classification.

Another common bias is what might be called the "hostility bias." In reading psychological reports, it has been the experience of many observers, along with Robinson and Cohen, that hostility, aggression, and various kinds of negative feelings on the part of the patient seem to be emphasized as opposed to passive pathology. This matter is discussed by Leary (16) who has invented such terms as "hypernormality" and "overconventionality" to indicate that people may be pathologically passive and conforming in their attitudes and behavior.

9
CASE OF MIKE

THE CASE OF MIKE* is intended to illustrate the process of integrating the results of a test battery. It can be seen that the whole (psychological report) is greater than the sum of its parts (interpretations of individual tests). The process of going from the concrete test data to the final conclusion is made explicit. No attempt was made to handle the separate tests blindly without knowledge of the case history or the other tests administered. Rather, each test was summarized in terms of the unique contributions it made to the understanding of the case. Since space does not justify presenting the complete protocol for each test, these have been recorded only when thought of the greatest interest. Test integration at the end is based upon a comparison of all the tests to each other and to the known case history. Interpretations and conclusions may be drawn from this over-all point of view which differ in emphasis or degree from individual interpretations of the tests themselves. A brief case history abstract is given containing the information available at the time this patient was tested. This information is about the same as that usually available under similar circumstances and is based upon an interview with the patient, summaries from the referring physician, and questionnaires filled out by the parents.

CASE HISTORY ABSTRACT

At the time Mike came to the State hospital, he was a tall, well-developed, white boy of 14, rather slender for his age with a rather defensive, arrogant manner. He was referred by a psychiatrist in private practice in the town where he resides.

Mike was born in a large midwestern city of parents who were 28 and 26. The father is an orphan of Irish extraction whose main interest

---

* This case was prepared in collaboration with Gertrude J. Williams and Earl S. Taulbee.

is music and who is currently employed as a clerk in the same organization as his wife, his superior in the work situation. He is described as a mild, happy-go-lucky individual who took little part in the discipline in the home. Mike's mother is of German extraction and is described as very uncompromising and harsh in her treatment of the patient. There is one sister, one year the patient's junior, of whom he is reported to be jealous.

Nothing is known about this boy until the age at which he started school. At this time it was noticed that he was considerably brighter than the average children in his class and excelled in his studies, but on the playground he tended to antagonize other children by his intellectual snobbishness. In those days the patient was rather frequently beaten by other children and had no friends at all. When asked how he felt about this, the patient said, "It didn't bother me; I just retreated to my books."

About a year ago, it was noticed that the patient was becoming increasingly deceitful, restless, nervous, and more arrogant. He made frequent derogatory remarks about his father's occupation and failures in life. Further, he would not accept discipline from his mother and on several occasions, slapped her face when she was remonstrating with him. During this period, the boy became increasingly interested in the German language and in German political systems, particularly National Socialism. He read voraciously the works of the major Nazi leaders and expressed regret that he was not a full-blooded German. He adopted many Nazi prejudices, being biased among other things against Negroes, Jews, Catholics, Communists, clergymen, women, and professional people. He says that he cares nothing about the United States but plans to emigrate to Germany at the first opportunity, there to participate in the resurgence of the Nazi movement and presumably become one of the leaders of the movement. Other ideas of his were even more farfetched, such as leading an expedition to Mars and taking it over.

In connection with his interest in things German, he took some German language courses at a local college and became very attached to his female German teacher. Also during this period the patient obtained a number which he calls his IQ. He constantly brings this into the conversation and seems to consider this allegedly superior IQ a very important part of his conscious self-concept.

The patient's course at the hospital was very stormy. He was very unhappy and dissatisfied with his surroundings, objecting especially to the caliber of the people he was forced to associate with, the menial tasks he was assigned, the food, the laundry, and everything else imaginable. He did not get along well with the other patients on the ward because of his arrogant attitude and his contempt for anyone not meeting his particular expectations of superior intelligence, sophisticated cultural background, etc.

He was treated by individual and group psychotherapy during his time in the hospital. He preferred not to consider himself an emotionally disturbed person who was in need of help, rather he made constant attempts to draw various staff members into discussions about his political ideas. He also attempted to impress them with other successes of his, such as creating a new language. He was most disagreeable towards other patients, saying that they were all morons, drunks, or slobs. He consistently told falsehoods to various staff members, attempting to set them against each other and make trouble in the institution.

His diagnostic studies included the various tests reported below. When admitted he was considered a diagnostic problem as there was insufficient evidence for a diagnosis. He was released after three months of hospitalization and referred for continued treatment to the out-patient facility of a city hospital.

Test Behavior

Mike was extremely cooperative during all test administrations, although toward the end of the battery he was able to verbalize some feelings of resentment regarding the examiner's "probing." He expressed hostility to all agencies and officials who were in any way connected with his hospitalization, and denied that his parents had any part in it. He declared that in a sense, he would be losing his "escutcheon" by being in a mental institution. He attempted to involve the examiner in a discussion of the pros and cons of Fascism, the inborn superiority of Aryans, and the inferiority of Jews and Negroes. Then, he began to cry and expressed regret that he had revealed so many of his opinions since he would be punished for them. When the examiner assured him that personal opinions did not influence professional decisions at the hospital, he appeared to be somewhat relieved, but skeptical. In general, while he accepted the necessity of testing, he did not feel this would be particularly useful since he felt his only problem was some of his "incorrect thinking."

Wechsler-Bellevue Intelligence Scale (Form I)

Subtest Scores

Information	15	Picture Arrangement	10
Comprehension	12	Picture Completion	9
Digit Span	16	Block Design	13
Arithmetic	13	Object Assembly	14
Similarities	16	Digit Symbol	7
Vocabulary	(12)		

Full Scale IQ	126
Verbal Scale IQ	139
Performance Scale IQ	107

Mike obtained a Full Scale IQ of 126, consisting of a verbal score of 139 and a performance score of 107. However, in spite of his superior intelligence, the large discrepancy between his verbal and performance scores (32 points) must be assumed to result from some special factors. Also, the marked superiority of the verbal IQ along with both the intra- and intersubtest scatter suggests an intellectualizing, obsessive tendency. For the most part, the patient gave no bizarre answers, nor was there much unusual verbalization or reasoning.

The fact that Mike has only one year of high school education and yet manages to obtain superior scores on at least three of the verbal subtests suggests that he is striving very hard toward intellectual achievement. Despite his limited education, he knows what the Koran is but says six pints make a quart. He first defines "ethnology" as the study of languages, then spontaneously corrects himself and says, "No, that's philology—ethnology is the study of human origin, the study of man."

Mike's unevenness of achievement is further manifested on the Comprehension subtest. On the relatively easy "theatre" item, he fails to score at all, missing the point of either notifying the responsible person or giving the alarm to the fire company instead of the audience. However, he gets full credit on the more difficult "deaf" item, again illustrating his greater ability to deal with the more abstract and less concrete and practical situations.

His scores on the Block Design, Object Assembly, Digit

Span, and Arithmetic subtests suggest that his intellectual functioning is not being seriously interfered with by any tension or anxiety. Either there is an absence of a significant amount of anxiety or he is successfully maintaining a superficially bland and unflustered approach.

Mike's intellectual functioning is more seriously disturbed on Performance tests than on Verbal ones. On the easy" ear" item of the Picture Completion subtest, he does not name the missing part, but instead describes the man as wearing lipstick. However, he correctly answers the most difficult item, the "shadow."

In Picture Arrangement his performance is somewhat better than the score would indicate since he gets the point of both the "fish" and "taxi" stories in 28 and 24 seconds respectively, but a minor error in sequence lowers his score on each from a maximum potential of 6 to 1.

In general, the Wechsler-Bellevue results indicate a very intelligent individual with some obsessive-compulsive features and a marked striving for intellectual and cultural achievement at the expense of inadequate attention to the practical and mundane matters of everyday living. His major defense appears to be that of intellectualization. It is likely that he appears to others as an ostentatious and ineffectual "intellectual."

There is a great deal that is unusual in Mike's performance on the Wechsler-Bellevue and certainly enough to suggest that he is not functioning in a healthy way. On the contrary, there are some paranoid schizophrenic features present which need further exploration. This is suggested by the marked discrepancy between the Verbal and Performance scores, in favor of the former; the high interest scatter within the Performance group; the low Picture Arrangement and Digit Symbol simultaneously with a high Digit Span score; a Digit Span score which is above the Information and Vocabulary (rather unusual except in some schizophrenic conditions); the relatively low Picture Arrangement and Picture Completion scores with the higher Block Design and Object Assembly; and a discrepancy between Information and Comprehension in favor of the former. All of these points would certainly suggest the possibility of paranoid schizophrenic involvement.

Benjamin's Proverbs

1. (When the cat's away, the mice will play.) "When authority is gone, other elements that are usually kept concealed are active or become active."

2. (Don't cry over spilt milk.) "Once a thing has been done, one shouldn't mourn about it, but if it's been done incorrectly, he should try to correct it."

3. (It never rains but it pours.) "Things usually don't happen in moderation but go to either extreme."

4. (The burnt child dreads the fire.) (Asks E. to repeat) "Once an unfortunate experience has happened to a person, that person subconsciously makes a mental note . . . now wait, let me get that again . . . that connects that . . . uh . . . unpleasant situation with the particular stimulus that causes it and thereon tries to avoid that particular stimulus."

5. (Don't cross your bridges till you come to them.) "That means one shouldn't get ahead of himself or . . . uh . . . take things as they come. It's the same as the proverb 'Don't count your eggs before they're hatched.' Another way of saying it is, 'Don't do things prematurely.'"

6. (A rolling stone gathers no moss.) "A rolling stone gathers no moss. That means to use an example, 'If you keep a certain machine working in top notch condition, which necessarily implies . . . uh . . . extremely good care, that machine will outlast one which has been only used infrequently and has been allowed to . . . uh . . . become defunct.'"

7. (Discretion is the better part of valor.) "I have to think of it because I have never understood it. That means, when you do something that of itself is of a great nature, that thing should be done with the utmost discretion or . . . in parentheses . . . not rashly, to insure the success of the project."

8. (To fiddle while Rome burns.) "That means, to look or stand idly by in a calm and composed mien . . . did I start the 'while' clause yet? . . . while something of great importance concerning you or possibly many other people in which you could have played a decisive part in the outcome . . . would you repeat that? . . . of the project is meanwhile occurring."

9. (Don't count your chickens until they're hatched.) "That means, don't act prematurely. It's almost the same as the one above. In fact, I think I even quoted that proverb."

10. (The proof of the pudding is in the eating.) "No matter what

things seem on the outside or what their appearance may be, the final good is proved through actual demonstration or use."

11. (He who laughs last, laughs best.) "Though in a business deal . . . this is an example . . . you may have been cheated . . . then semicolon . . . later you may have the opportunity to return the misdeed with all justice, thereby having the last laugh. 'Last laugh' is in quotation marks."

12. (New brooms sweep clean.) "A thing, when it is usually new . . . that's the wrong sentence order . . . a thing usually when it's new functions more properly than when after it's put to repeated use."

13. (Ingratitude, thy name is woman.) "According to that proverb, which sounds more like a personal opinion than a fact, women are portrayed to be notoriously ingratuous."

14. (He travels swiftest who travels alone.) "Sometimes extra company, like extra baggage, can weight a talented person down."

Mike claimed that he "heard all of the proverbs before but couldn't put them all at my fingertips." He then contradicted himself and said that he had not heard proverbs 8, 9, 10, 11, 12, and 13. He claimed to have heard a version of 14, saying "'the best wolf is a lone wolf,' which means exactly the same thing."

Mike's interpretation of the proverbs ranged from complete literalness to false symbolization. His frequent literalness and concrete approach are often veiled by overintellectualization and pseudo-abstraction. On the other hand, he goes beyond the proverb, investing it with complex-determined content, compulsively attempting to exhaust the potentialities of the proverbs. While Mike does demonstrate some capacity to shift from literalness to abstraction, this shift is more a reflection of the instability of his own formal thinking than of critical evaluation of the proverbs themselves. He is literal where abstraction is necessary; he overabstracts when he should be concrete. Such a disturbance in formal thought and the overelaborate use of language as well as the content of some of his complex-determined responses appear to be in keeping with those found in paranoid schizophrenia.

Summary of Vigotsky Performance

This test presented very little difficulty to Mike. Though he initially stated that he was not very adept, he was able to get the major principle after very little preliminary trial and error behavior. He grasped the concept of size differences immediately, rejected color and shape hypotheses without trying them out, and correctly divided the blocks in a total of 15 minutes time. The interpretation is that this task, because of its impersonal nature, was not interfered with by the patient's difficulties in verbal generalizations. This test can be contrasted with his performance on the Benjamin Proverbs.

Forer Sentence Completion Test

Mike's spontaneous responses to the sentences were with one word. After sentence 41,*† the examiner asked him if he knew he did not have to confine himself to one word. Mike said that he had understood these instructions but had thought that one word was sufficient. The examiner administered the remainder of the test and readministered items 2 to 41.‡ The item administered is in all capitals, Mike's responses are in lower case letters.

2. HE OFTEN WISHED HE COULD live. (die)
5. WHEN SHE REFUSED HIM, HE cried. (kicked her)
6. I USED TO FEEL I WAS BEING HELD BACK BY it. (my teacher)
8. AS A CHILD MY GREATEST FEAR WAS them. (them)
10. MEN—what?—are. (are arrogant)
12. I WAS MOST DEPRESSED WHEN I. (I got beat up)
16. MOST FATHERS are. (kind)
19. I COULD HATE A PERSON WHO did. (betray me or lied to me too)
21. WHEN I MEET A WOMAN, I—can't think—cried. (blush)
24. WHEN I THINK BACK, I AM ASHAMED THAT we. (it was done)
25. IF I THINK THE JOB IS TOO HARD FOR ME, I quit. (fight)
26. SISTERS are. (are nice)
28. WHEN THEY TALKED ABOUT SEX, I listened. (was fairly interested)
29. I USED TO DAY DREAM ABOUT him. (nothing)

* Numbers refer to selected items from Forer's Sentence Completion Test.

† It might have been better to have completed the test administration and then readministered the test with the suggestion that one-word answers were not a necessity.

‡ Words in parentheses refer to responses to readministration.

31. WHEN I HAVE TO MAKE A DECISION, I think. (I think)
32. LOVE IS foolish. (worthwhile in some situations)
34. I WAS MOST ANNOYED WHEN she. (I was held back)
36. TAKING ORDERS is. (is pleasing)
37. I DISLIKE TO do that. (kill)
38. I FEEL THAT PEOPLE look. (dislike him)
39. MOST WOMEN think. (are vain)
40. AFTER HE MADE LOVE TO HER, HE died. (died)
41. IF I CAN'T GET WHAT I WANT, I fight. (struggle)
45. I USED TO FEEL "DOWN IN THE DUMPS" WHEN I was cheated.
46. WHEN THEY DIDN'T INVITE ME, I felt bad, I was angry.
49. A LOT OF PEOPLE are nice.
50. BROTHERS are understanding.
52. MOST OF ALL I WANT position.
58. MOST MARRIAGES are happy.
60. MY MOTHER is nice.
62. RESPONSIBILITY I love.
64. SHE FELT BLUE WHEN he kicked her.
66. WHEN I MEET PEOPLE, I GENERALLY FEEL proud.
68. WHEN THEY PUT ME IN CHARGE, I feel happy.
70. WHEN MY FATHER CAME HOME, I met him.
74. I FEEL HAPPIEST WHEN it happened.
76. WHEN MY MOTHER CAME HOME, I greeted her.
77. WHEN THEY TOLD HIM WHAT TO DO, HE was mad.
79. HER GREATEST WORRY WAS him.
81. MOST WOMEN ACT AS THOUGH they are beasts.
82. WHEN I FEEL THAT OTHERS DON'T LIKE ME, I hate 'em.
84. MOST PEOPLE ARE nice.
86. I COULD LOSE MY TEMPER IF somebody double crossed me.
87. I AM AFRAID OF spiders.
89. A MAN WOULD BE JUSTIFIED IN BEATING A WO-MAN WHO betrayed him.
91. SOMETIMES I FEEL THAT MY BOSS is justified in his actions.
92. WHEN I THINK OF MARRIAGE, I shudder.
95. MOST MEN ACT AS THOUGH they are better.
96. FATHERS are stern.
100. I FEEL SAD ABOUT death.

Method of data analysis followed that of Forer (8). Mike's initial response to the test with one word is consistent with a psychotic process. Such sentence completion as no. 16 ". . . FATHERS are," or no. 36 "TAKING ORDERS is," while apparently satisfactory to him, are distortions of the structural reality of the sentences. At this time at least, his associative process seemed blocked and language was not used for communicative purposes.

In terms of content, Mike's responses indicate the strong affect associated with his attitudes towards women in both his expressed anxiety, sentence 5, his paucity of associations, sentence 26, and his later noncommittal response suggest that his relationship with his sister is problematical. In regard to his attitudes towards male figures, his initial responses to nos. 10 and 16 and his later contradictory responses suggest the strength of his ambivalence in this area. Further conflict is reflected in his attitude toward authority, which is generally passive (36 and 91), and toward assuming the responsiblity which he claims to enjoy (77, 62, 68).

In terms of his own needs, his ambivalence toward keeping up the struggle is reflected, but the question must be raised as to whether life is so unbearable to him that it actually is equated with death (2). There is some suggestion of repressed homosexual impulses (29) and extreme aggression which he must reject (37).

In general a lack of integrity on the part of another person provokes his aggression (19, 86). Aggression, in turn, appears to be equated with depression (12, 45, 64). This trend is borne out by his responses to both 5 and to 46. He is angry when he is sad; he is sad when he is angry. An evaluation of his aggressive responses reveal that this equation may be due to his strong intrapunitive tendencies. He attempts to turn his aggression inward, but failing this, he must act them out completely. There is no middle ground, and his strong aggressive impulses are not channelized.

Another trend is suggested in no. 40 where love and death are associated, with the implication that heterosexuality may be a dangerous act. He views marriage as a mixture of foolishness, happiness, and fear, again revealing his marked uncertainty and ambivalence (32, 58, 92).

Summary of Rosenzweig P-F Study

Mike's performance on the Rosenzweig appears consistent with the kind of picture that he was trying to give of himself when he first entered the hospital. His most characteristic response was a persistent intrapunitive need. Next in order of frequency were impunitive-ego defensive responses, ego defensive-extrapunitive responses. Most of his reactions to the situations were in terms of trying to gloss over the frustrating situation, take the blame himself, and at the same time continue to work for what he wanted. The results of this test are quite radically at variance with the clinical impression and with the results of many of his other tests. The fact that he was here behaving in a socially acceptable manner is further illustrated by the fact that 70 per cent of his responses were of the popular variety. The examiners felt that Mike's Rosenzweig P-F study may reflect a superficial aspect of his functioning rather than any basic attitude or behavioral characteristics.

Minnesota Multiphasic Personality Inventory

Scale	T-Score	Scale	T-Score
?	50	Pd	55
L	50	Mf	52
F	45	Pa.	50
K	63	Pt.	44
Hs	52	Sc	53
D	55	Ma	42
Hy	62		

An analysis of the MMPI suggests that the patient was quite defensive. He placed 27 of the cards in the "cannot say" category, several of which contribute to the validity scales.

The MMPI pattern per se does not reveal a great deal about the individual. It suggests that he has a strong ego and has repressed his affect. A content analysis of the record indicates that he was unable to answer many of the items concerning religion and his relationship with the members of his family.

He appears to be rather hostile toward and suspicious of people, and there is considerable phobic material present. It is felt that these areas are the ones in which there is the greatest disturbance and that he, consciously or unconsciously, was very evasive and defensive concerning them. He does not appear to be psychotic, but it is not unlikely that there are some anxiety and conversion features in the personality.

Blacky Test

CARTOON I (Ora. Ero.): "I suppose that Blacky has just been born and after he's been born he's nursing milk from his mother."

Inquiry: 1, a; 2, b; 3, b; 4, b; 5, a; 6, a.

CARTOON II (Ora. Sad.): "I suppose Blacky has found his mama's collar on the ground and is just shaking it. He is shaking the collar on the ground like dogs often do playfully."

Inquiry: 1, "Just playfully." 2, c; 3, c; 4, a; 5, a; 6, b.

CARTOON III (Ana. Sad.): "Oh, Blacky's relieving himself and is digging with his paws like dogs do after they do that."

Inquiry: 1, c; 2, b; 3, c. 4, "That's silly, there's only one possible answer, a." 5, "That he's been a good dog for being . . . doing what he's been taught." 6, "Papa will repeat the same thing."

CARTOON IV (Oed. Int.): "I don't see why he's growling there myself. I don't understand. (Pause) Since he is such a young dog— young people or dogs get jealous of the attention mother is giving his father naturally."

Inquiry: 1, "Well, looks like he's jealous." (*Why?*)* "Because of the attention thing. Perhaps he doesn't like his father's attention, or the mother's too." (I.e., M or P's attention to each other.) 2, c; 3, b. 4, d "In Blacky's case." 5, "Nothing." (I.e., P will do nothing.) 6, "The same." (I.e., M will do nothing.) 7, "Neither one. Couldn't I say 'a' and 'b'? Somebody is being deprived any way you look at it and that wouldn't be right. Families should be mutual. Mama and papa weren't trying to be selfish."

CARTOON V (Mas. Glt.): "Well, I don't see that part of it. He is cleaning himself. That is the natural thing for any dog to do. It wouldn't have sexual implications, I wouldn't think."

Inquiry: 1, "I might be a problem child, but none are right. It's a funny slant." (*Q*) "Well, he's merely doing what he's been taught again. There's nothing to be guilty, ashamed or happy about. He's just cleaning himself, there is no ulterior motive here." 2, "The same

_____
* Throughout examiners questions will be indicated by italics.

as one." 3, "Could be anybody, but his thoughts wouldn't be connected with the act he is doing right now most likely." 4, "No" 5, "She'll probably praise him for his cleanliness." 6, "Same for father."

CARTOON VI (Cas. Anx.): "Well, I suppose Tippy's getting her tail cut off to prevent germs. The tail sometimes drags in the dirt and picks up dirt, etc. There is nothing cruel about it. That isn't how they cut them off. If Blacky is an intelligent dog, he is watching with as much glee as possible because he realizes that maybe someday it will happen to him then, as it is a favor to Tippy now. He is actually realizing that this is the best thing and a profit for him to have it done too."

Inquiry: 1, c; 2, c. 3, "It's slightly c." 4, "If he's a smart dog." (*Why?*) "The advantages to a dog to have its tail cut off and the little pain it causes him, may save his life later on—from picking up some sort of disease." 5, "If the ideal family, both mother and father conjunctively would have seen to that." 6, d "But they won't admire him because he's brave enough to have it cut off, but smart enough to have it cut off, thereby protecting himself for later."

CARTOON VII (Pos. Ide.) "I don't know what he would be doing. Oh, he must be jealous of it and mad and is sticking out his tongue and waving his hands around. That's what he's doing—waving his finger around emphatically for it to answer, but since it's wood, it can't answer and he's getting madder and madder. That was a long one."

Inquiry: 1, "None of them." (*Q*) "I don't think mama and papa would talk to him like that. It's not fair to say they do when they don't, they would when they wouldn't." 2, "He should obey mama or papa both together. He shouldn't take one over the other. If it is controversial, they should decide together, not order him around." 3, "Well, he might . . . oh, I don't know. If it's anybody . . . it could possibly be Tippy when a baby, but not mama or papa cause they'd have sense enough not to act like that. He might just be playing too." 4, "Blacky is a boy, isn't he? If he is a boy he would pattern himself after papa, and if a girl, after mama." 5, "In general, he's not like any of them. In that picture it's the babyish attitude of Tippy, because Tippy is younger in my mind." 6, b "In the sense he would ignore it. Just ignore it not stand there and look stupid. Ignoring it is different from standing there and taking it."

CARTOON VIII (Sib. Riv.): "Oh, I suppose Blacky is sort of jealous, although he shouldn't be because mama and papa bestow the same affection on him, but he doesn't remember it. He's stupid, stupid if he's jealous. You might say, he's curious. If he's a good dog, he'd only be curious."

Inquiry: 1, b. 2, a "It depends on what Tippy's done." 3, c; 4, a. 5, b "Should be." 6, "It's not jealousy. He's most mad at Tippy. Tippy might have done something, but might have merited mama and papa's praise. Blacky might have slandered them, lied, you know, and it's actually not his fault."

(*Note:* Several days later the patient referred to the card and said that he had been thinking about the test and this card in particular. He said that naturally, anybody would tell a story about jealousy to this card.)

CARTOON IX (Glt. Fee.): (Laughs) "That's a fine lookin' angel if I ever saw one. It doesn't look like an angel at all. It shouldn't have a halo, it should have horns. If an angel came down at me, bearing its teeth at me, I'd be afraid too. But if it's a nice angel *Tippy* wouldn't have any excuse to be afraid."

Inquiry: 1, "Tippy might have gone off some . . . Blacky . . . place to pout about it—*if* he were angry." 2, "Well, I don't know what the conscience is trying to do. The conscience is needlessly cruel to him. If the conscience reprimanded him, that would be different, but it just came down and scared him. It is better to have no conscience at all than a conscience like that." 3, "You mean mama, papa, or Tippy? Maybe something like doom or something. All I can say is that it's the worst looking angel. It's slander to put a halo over its head." 4, a "If he went and sulked in a corner it's his own fault." 5, a "If he sulked in a corner. I think he's just scared, not guilty." 6, "I don't know if he's done something wrong he might beg for forgiveness. If it just came down and scared him, he'd beg for mercy. You know, 'don't hit me.' Something like that." 7, c.

CARTOON X (Pos. Eg. Id.): "I suppose he dreams of himself—you know, like a knight on a shining horse, the aristocrat of dogs. Some hunting dog, something like that."

Inquiry: 1, "It might remind him of his father. His father is not black though. He might be placing himself in father's place. He admires father very much. I'm supposed to be Blacky, aren't I?" 2, "The way papa's been acting and he's been acting nice, I think he would. That doesn't answer it. He stacks up to it fine." 3, c "Possibly, maybe d, or if I were in his place, I'd be handsome just for the sake of being handsome. Pride in myself to be nice looking." 4, a "He's a little conceited." 5, b; 6, c.

CARTOON XI (Lv. Obj.): "Oh, I suppose he's dreaming of his . . . either his girl friend or his mother. Maybe an idealized shot . . . thought of his mother, what he'd like mama to be. No, not what he'd like mama to be actually. Well, I guess that's it. If he could have his own way. Or a girl friend when he's a knight."

Inquiry: 1, "Either mama or a girl friend." 2, "Same." 3, b or c "Equally so, it depends on his state of mind." 4, "I don't know. He didn't look contented to me. When you dream, you're not especially happy. You just dream. None of them are right. Just that he likes to dream about something he would admire, a thing of beauty." 5, "Same thing as with papa. If mama has been nice to him, and from all apparent reasons it looks as if she has, then it would stack up." 6, "No. He's a man, that's a woman on that."

CARTOON PREFERENCES: Likes: I, IV, V, VI, VIII, X, XI. In reference to card V, he says, "That one's cleaning himself, there is no undercurrent. It's just that he's cleaning himself and being cleanly." Dislikes II, III, VII, IX. One liked best, VIII. "No unpleasant undercurrent at all. Everybody's face is smiling. I can't see his face whether he's smiling or not." One liked least, IX. "I don't like the expression on that horrible thing's face. It isn't even a fair conscience. A conscience is supposed to be strict but that's mean, not strict."

Family Information: Father, living, age 42; mother, living, age 41; siblings, a sister, age 13.

Because of the brevity and the noncommittal nature of Mike's stories and his not making a choice on several of the inquiry items, the following interpretation is of necessity limited to certain aspects of the personality which are revealed in the qualitative nuances of the protocol and should be considered only as suggestive and not definitive.

The Blacky record reveals a very strong defense system, largely comprised of such mechanisms as denial, repression, and intellectualization. Mike manifests a constant denial and reaction formation in order to maintain repression of the affect associated with his anxiety-provoking impulses and ideas. The occasional breaking through of phobic material illustrates the ineffectual nature of this repression. Sibling rivalry, jealousy, and hostility are fairly strong but are deeply repressed, as is his oedipal involvement. It appears that he has resolved or is currently in the process of resolving many of his adolescent conflicts.

Mike manifests some confusion in sexual identification and sometimes feels that feminity is less threatening and dangerous than is masculinity. At times, it appears as though he is seeking castration because of his underlying anxiety. Masturbatory guilt and anxiety are present, and consequently, there is probably avoidance of masturbatory behavior. Mike has a strong need to play a conforming role, to be a "good boy."

The presence of oral dependent needs is suggested and while they are not strong on a normative basis, they may be disturbing to him. Although he fears his own conscience, he is more afraid of external punishment and refuses to reveal the threatening or punishing agent.

Make A Picture Story Test

During the administration of this test, Mike grouped all the Negro figures together and asked the examiner about her religion.

LIVING ROOM: "He's just coming in the door." (Places figures M10 and F6 on background.) "Wait, I'll change that." (Substitutes figure F8.) "I don't have to put a lot of people in here, do I? She should be facing him. Dad comes home real happy." (Places C1 carelessly.) "Mom is standing there with a frown on her face. The daughter has done something wrong, and the daughter's ashamed. I'll put the dog in there." (Adds A1.) "She doesn't know what's going to go on there." (*What is the outcome?*) "She'll apologize to Daddy; run over and cry on his shoulder. Daddy will say it's all right. Mom was just mad when he came in the door. She's not mad at the little girl, just what the little girl did. A lot of families, they like the husband to take authority; the mother is just lovey dovey in any case."

STREET: (Places all figures on background.) "A man is hit by a car, and these two women, one is holding her hand to her face in horror and the other is doing approximately the same thing." (*What is the outcome?*) "Both women will scream and walk away after the body is taken away."

MEDICAL: "Either this" (Places C5) "or this" (Places F1). "Either one of those are waiting for an operation. I don't see any doctors about. Well, this could sort of be a doctor, calm." (Places M15 carelessly.) "Maybe he's not giving an operation. They're probably just taking an examination."

BATH ROOM: (Places M1, C6, C5, F1 in that order.) "It could be any of these four here. They're about ready to use—to take a bath."

DREAM: (Places all figures on background as follows: A2, L4, L6, L5, M4.) "This man is picturing what he might be, and on this side, he's having a nightmare." (Adds figure L1.) "He might even picture

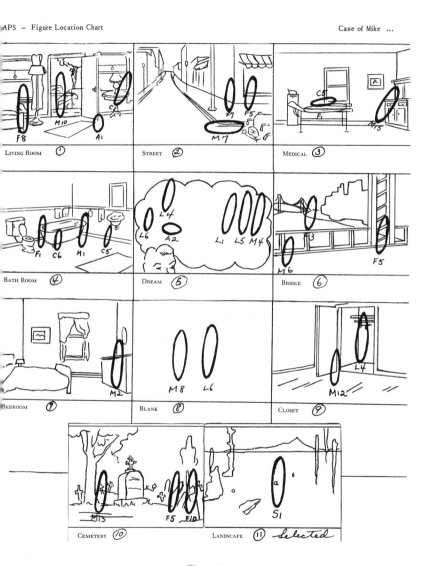

Figure 1

MAPS—Figure Location Chart

himself as a king. Here he's pointing down for someone to polish his boots for him. You know, being stinky about it." (*What will the outcome be?*) "These three are what he might be; these three are night-mares." (Laughs) "Oh, he probably goes back to his little $35 a week book counting job the morning after his dream."

BRIDGE: (Places F5, F3, M6 in that order.) "That man is trying to force that girl to jump off that bridge there, and one woman is holding her hand in front of her face there. Maybe she's screaming." (*What will the outcome be?*) "Oh, I suppose the policeman would either shoot the man or stop him. Her screams bring the police. She tries to help if she's exceptionally brave. If she's exceptionally brave, she probably wouldn't scream. She'd stop him in the interests of humanity. I should find a policeman, but none are running; they're all standing at atten-tion." (*What is the man's motivation?*) "You never can tell. It may be a jealous husband or revenge for something she did—one of his ac-quaintances. Just that he doesn't like her for some reason."

BEDROOM: "Somebody's already there in bed. Well, this could be in it too." (Places M2.) "It could be a room shared by two people. That's somebody's head there. The man's just undressing preparatory to going to bed. He's tired and wants to go to bed." (*What are his thoughts and feelings?*) "His utmost thought is that he would like to get his clothes off as that would hinder his sleeping." (*Who might the figure in bed be?*) "It doesn't look like a woman; it must be another man. Probably." (Yawns.) "Sometimes in college, they have rooms where two people bed together."

BLANK: "Okey, I'll use my imagination. I entitle this one, Dialogue. It's just the dialogue between some sort of . . . somebody from a re-ligious affiliation . . . a monk. No, it isn't because the hair isn't shaved off. It's a priest because of his sloppy clothes. The other is some sort of friend from Gehenna, another word for under the ground." (*What are they talking about?*) "I don't know. It seems like I read a book, 'A Dialogue in Hades or Purgatory.' That's why it's a dialogue. They even go together." (*What is the outcome?*) "I can't explain it. I'm just enchanted with the title, but I've never been able to get my hands on the book."

CLOSET: I've never heard of anybody hanging white shirts in the closet, but maybe that's what he's doing. There's an old ghost in the closet. I suppose the man was taking his shirt off and opened the closet door and finds a ghost there. It floated through the wall. It's just kind of giving him a little bit of a scare just for the fun of it. The guy runs out of the house scared. Or if he's sensible, he'd just stay there. If a ghost can go through a wall, it doesn't have any substance; if it doesn't have any substance, how can it touch you, if there's no substance?"

CEMETERY: "There's an Irish cross and a Jewish star; they'd have to have that in there. I'll assemble all the grieving mothers here." (Places F5 and F10.) "Well, this one old lady; when he was alive, he gave her some coins and she is one of the few to mourn. This one's trying to hold back a sob. This guy's got his head bowed." (Adds M13.) "Maybe this woman's his wife. This is probably his father; he's an older man." (*What happens next?*) "Oh, they cry for a little and then go back home."

(Patient is asked to select one of the remaining backgrounds to tell a story about, selects landscape.)

LANDSCAPE: "This one's a pretty picture." (Places S1.) "This is just a nameless figure reaching for the sun, you know. It's not just a person; it could be a symbol. Science, searching for the truth. It's just the relative truth in our times. A symbol for the act of going forward, going to attain higher goals."

In purely formal terms, Mike gets a score of 12 according to Shneidman's (21) "schizophrenic signs." He also gives a great many "normal signs." However, the careless placement of his figures on their background (C1 in Living Room, M15 in Medical scene) as well as the spacial inappropriateness (C5 and F1 in Medical scene and possibly F3 in the Bridge scene) suggest a loosening of reality ties. Mike's "sign" count points to a borderline level of reality functioning: he is certainly far from a good adjustment, but he cannot be considered overtly schizophrenic.

In terms of the stories themselves, Mike's views toward men and women are dichotomous: woman are emotional and men are rational. This is exemplified by the Living Room scene where "the husband takes authority, the women are lovey-dovey." In general, however, women's emotional expressions are considered neither effective nor genuine. After they have cried out in fear or sadness, they merely walk away. Their emotional expression brings them exactly nothing except, possibly, temporary relief.

In the sexual sphere, the Medical scene suggests a possible association of sexuality with aggression. This is implied by Mike's need to change the doctor's activity from surgery to merely an examination of the inappropriately placed naked woman and the child. The Bedroom scene has implications for homosexual impulses in Mike's making the sleeping figure another man, in spite of his attempt at justifying this in reality terms.

Mike's problem of emotionality versus intellectualism finds fullest expression in his story on the Blank card. He chooses figures not usually peopling his world and the general theme is one with which he is probably preoccupied at present. There is actually no story, merely a setting where symbols of good and evil, the rational and irrational, have a dialogue. His dream story reflects another schism: both the gratification and the fears associated with his phantasy. The monsters peopling his dreams suggest that phantasy is not completely satisfying to him at present. However, even the reality to which he eventually wakens is mediocre and barren.

His vague reality ties are demonstrated in his Closet story where he is more critical about the possibility of hanging a white shirt in the closet than about the appropriateness of discovering a ghost there. In addition, he selects the isolated Landscape background to tell a story of truth, "not just people."

His inability to deal with "just people" is reflected in his Bridge story where he reveals his utterly inappropriate methods of handling his aggression. In this story, the man forces the woman to jump, rather than pushing her off. This compromise relieves him of the responsibility of his aggressiveness. His resort to intellectualization and to symbols again shows itself in the woman's screaming in the interests of humanity, rather than for the sake of the hapless girl. The strength of motivation in this story gradually diminishes until we find that the man is committing these aggressive acts because "he doesn't like her." In short, Mike is a boy whose level of emotional integration is poor, who attempts to intellectualize as a defense against ego-alien impulses such as aggression and sexuality, and whose reality ties are certainly in the process of weakening.

RORSCHACH RECORD

CARD I (Initial time 4", total time 1' 15")
1. Well, I see some animal. Kind of a lion with wings. A griffin. It could have been a sphinx the way the legs are spread

apart. That kind of stance. It could have been a horse, but it seemed like a winged lion at first.

Score: D   F>FM   (A)

2.V A crocodile spread out maybe. Maybe just his skin.

It didn't look lifelike. It looked kind of flat. There's no depth, like a skin wouldn't have depth. It could have been any other animal up to this part, the mouth. It could have been a crocodile, but its mouth is broader.

Score: dr   F   Aobj

3. Two open hands sticking out sideways.

The head, with kind of like a hood over it. It looks like human hands. They're looking straight into each others eyes. (Demonstrates head and hand position.) (*Male or female?*) I can't tell. There's nothing there to indicate that.

Score: d   M   Hd

4.V The head of an aborigine with fuzzy hair.

Like they have in Australia. The jagged edges look like hair. Not like a Negro. The features aren't strong enough. You know how Negroes have those big noses.

Score: d   F   Hd

5.V The head and neck of an eagle.

The neck, head and . . . doesn't look quite like an eagle. When I first looked at it, it looked like an eagle, but it's too broad here. I still say it's an eagle even though it doesn't look like it. It seems like it.

Score: d   F   Ad

6.V The head of a rooster; he's got his beak in something. I could tell it's a rooster because it has waddles.

These are the waddles and this is the something he's gotten into and this is the neck.

Score: dr   FM   Ad

CARD II (Initial time 6'', total time 2' 3'')

1. Well, it looks like two people playing patty-cake. They're shaggy. Looks like claws on their feet. The top part of their head is stretched out narrow. Their teeth are sticking out, and there's a point for an eye. The shoulder blades stick out.

It's a shaggy color, the grey. It's sloppy and dirty. Here are their elongated heads. Where it's irregular are the claws. They're kind of kneeling and both hands are like that. I don't know what to call that. It's some sort of stance. (Demonstrates.) One knee sticks up behind it. This could be their navel. (*Male or female?*) Men. Well, they look kinda like . . .

you know, women. It depends on how you look at it. It could be men or a woman who talks all the time from that mouth.

Score: W   M,FC'   (H)

2.V This red thing looks like some sort of spiny thing in the sea. It has hard spines all over.

This part is smoother. There's no jagged outline. It's kinda reddish grey. It could be a transparent animal. (*Red?*) Things in the sea are usually a bright color.

Score: D   Fc,F/C   A
add.   D   F   (Hd)

add. I see something I didn't see before. It looks like a human face but shaggy like an ape. It has a back like a baboon with no hair, a hump on its back like a camel. The nose is hooked, human. Like a Jewish nose. Like a hooked beak.

3.V Also, it looks like two little animals, and they've got a hand open behind them and a single horn on top of their heads and a shorter horn.

If this little pinkish area in the middle is included, then it's that spiny thing. But if you leave it out, then it's the two little animals. They kinda have a little nose. It's like a dog with jowls that hang down. The mouth. Is this the one I said looked like a shmoo? This looks like a shmoo. Here are the little legs at the bottom. They're in sort of a gesture.

Score: D   F>M   (Ad)

4. The head of an octopus.

There's sort of a hooked thing on both sides. It doesn't really look like a head, but sort of. It's like looking down on it. There's sort of a crest that divides him.

Score: D   F,Fc   Ad

CARD III (Initial time 6", total time 1' 57")

1. O.k., this looks like two ant-people maybe. Some sort of insect because the mouth looks like an insect's with all the little things in it.

The body, chest or breast, neck, head. The reason they look like ant-people is that the mouth is like an ant's. They're separated here, but here starts their leg. (*Male or female?*) I don't know. In a way, they're female; in a way, they're male. Perhaps they combine the characteristics of both. (*What way?*) The breasts make it a woman. Other than that, they just look generally like men. (*How seen?*) I can hardly describe it. The back is crooked. They're bending down with their arms parallel.

Score: W̶ M   (H)P add. O-

2. Two beans connected by a little tube.

> Kidney beans. They could be lima beans too, but just the general outline of a bean. Color didn't have anything to do with it. They're on display so that both sides of the bean can be seen. Just something somebody drew or put on display. The tube shows they are parts of the same bean.

Score: D   F   Pl

3. Some sort of animal falling. The jaw sticks out further and the forehead is protruding. On its back it's got something that looks like a tail and little teeny wings.

> With the mother's tube on it if it's an unborn baby. Something like that. Kinda human and kinda like an ape. The jaw sticks out but it has a delicate nose. The forehead slopes back like a primitive man.

Score: D   Fm   (H)

4. Then there is a crab.

> Just the shape.

Score: D   F   A

5. Then there's two hands stretched out with the palms open like they want something. (Referring to response 1.) Those ant people look like they have big plant lice attached to their hands.

> The palms are up and they're human. (*What in the card suggests plant lice to you?*) It's just the shape of plant lice.
>
> *add.* V The plant lice upside down look like a Negro man with bushy beard and a real scrawny neck. The arm is pointing back to itself. The arm is way twisted over with the thumb up. Kinda looks like he's got his mouth open, saying, "Who, me?" (Demonstrates.) (*Negro?*) It just looks kinda shaggy. You know how they look, the broad nose.

Score: d   M   Hd
add.   dr   M   H

CARD IV (Initial time 2'', total time 1' 3'')

1.V Looks like the head of a squid with big wings on it, and on the end of each wing is a . . .

> Eyes. Kinda black. Makes it look like eyes.

Score: dr   F   Ad

2. Dog's head with the mouth open. Here are the eyes and I can see the eyes of the squid.

> (*Responses 1 and 2 separate?*) They could have been. I just meant that the dog's head is at the end of the wings. But I

considered it separate. It's a regular old dog with its mouth open. Kind of yapping like.

Score: d   FM   Ad

3. On the side is an old man with a funny nose.

Here's the hood, an old-time cap, kind of a cap. A little turned-up nose, a little chin. Could be a wolf's head cap like primitive people wore. You take a wolf, skin it and with the skin coming down behind, you slip under the skin and stick your face through it.

Score: d   F   Hd/Ad   O

4. And the longer part of the head of a goose.

The beak, eye and neck. Looks like when it's dead. Just slumped over, hanging over dead. Bending double like. This could be his foot.

Score: d   F,Fm   A

5. Then there's a white ghost head.

The eye and nose. No body, just a vague outline.

Score: S   FC'   (Hd)

6. That looks like one of those shmoo things.

Just the shape.

Score: dr   F   (A)

7. The end here looks like skin, shrivelled skin or something.

It's wrinkled. (*What in the card suggests skin to you?*) It's smooth, but it's still wrinkled. It's like folded over, lighter inside. Kind of a hole.

add. It seems like the earth's crust like it's seen from an airplane.

add. There's lava. It looks like beds of lava. When it curls, it all wrinkles up.

Score: d   cF   At
add.   d   FK   N
add.   d   cF   N

CARD V (Initial time 2", total time 55")

1. That looks kinda like a butterfly or a bat with its big wings. On one side looks like a bat because of small feelers.

V A butterfly's antenna's skinny. This bat's got definite lines.

Score: W   F   A   P

2. The other side looks like a butterfly because of the big feelers. Looks like a moth or butterfly.

May be a moth because of the little feelers.

Score: W   F   A

3. On the ends of the wings, I can see a crocodile head.

> The eye. The mouth is open smiling. Kind of like a smirk there.

> *add.* Here's a baby's face with a turned-up nose, curly hair, the eye. The mouth is open. It's monkeylike. Not a very cute kid.

Score: d   FM>M   Ad
add.   dr   M   Hd

CARD VI (Initial time 2'', total time 1' 7'')

1. That looks like spread wings that are kind of frayed, of a grasshopper when it's flying. The head and mouth.

> The mottled part of the wings. (Indicates shading in side D.) Mouth and eyes. It's got its back, its stomach to me. The mouth and the two eyes looking down at you.

Score: D   FM,Fc   A

2. Two little bears back to back, and they have beards like Egyptian Pharoahs. They're metallic looking. Both have breasts and their legs are small. They have curly hair on top.

> Kind of playful like bears. The arm and leg. (*Metallic?*) I had a predetermined concept that they weren't of hair but of metal. They're kind of stiff and got their arm out like that. (Demonstrates.) It could be a statue.

Score: D   F>FM   A>Hd

3. And they have dog's heads on their arms.

> Nose, eyes, and mouth. (*Kind?*) Just a general dog. With its mouth shut for a change. I always see them with their mouths open, but I finally got his shut.

Score: d   F   Ad

4. Between the heads are two hooded figures that are brandishing knives.

> Like they're facing each other. They've got knives over their heads. (*Male or female?*) I couldn't tell. It just shows the head. The hood covers the face completely like the Ku Klux Klan. How do you analyze these?

Score: d   M   Hd

CARD VII (Initial time 3'', total time 52'')

1. Looks like two people facing each other, like babies because their foreheads are receding and they have big holes for eyes. Hands are behind them. No legs. The bottom part of the body just comes together. A long loop, not a loop, a handle of hair on their heads.

It doesn't look like it's receding, it looks like it's protruding. Like the Moslems who shave off their hair except for one lock of hair that Mohammed pulls you up to heaven by.

add. Looks like two women acting smart-alecky in a pose like that. (Puts hand on hip.) A superior pose.

add. There are faces all along there in profile. This one's forehead makes this one's lips and so forth.

add. This looks like some kind of insect. It's got its wings completely pulled off and just got the body left.

Score: W M H

 add. W M H
 add. de F Hd
 add. d F (Ad)

CARD VIII (Initial time 3'', total time 1' 18'')

1. Looks like two hyenas walking, kinda looking down at something.

Looks like they're on the prowl. They're looking for some dead meat, something defenseless.

Score: D FM A P

2. On the side is a camel's head.

I don't know what a camel's head looks like. It has a stupid grin on it and a hump on its back.

Score: d FM>M Ad

3. On the side is the head of a frog.

It looks kinda contented. It looks like it's enjoying itself to the utmost.

add. It could be a cow maybe. The low part if the mouth is smiling and contented. Like the company says, "Contented cows." Just chawing on cut grass. It's eyes are closed.

Score: D M Ad

 add. D FM>M Ad

4. Some sort of cross between a spider and a—something like a spider.

It reminds me of a spider but it doesn't look like it. All those legs. I was first going to say "centipede" but it didn't look like it. There's its beak.

Score: D F A add. O-

5. Then two flags of blue. (Referring to response 2.) That camel's got—a big inflated chest. This sticks out further than the chest. The lower part of the back is out as far as the chest, pronounced as much as the chest.

Crossed flags.

Score: D FC obj.

CARD IX (Initial time 2'', total time 1' 43'')

1. Looks like two old men with pot bellies facing each other. Points on their heads are like a gnome's. A tusk coming out of their mouth.

It's like antlers. There's the breast. The antler is growing out of their mouths. (*Male or female?*) Oh, I don't know. When you see an old potbellied thing, you don't think of women.

Score: D   F>M   H   add. O-

2. On the side is a green person with a mouth like a hog. He has a bump on his back and he's sucking his finger.

Looks like he's kissing the sea horse. Judge a piggish animal. Not necessarily green, with big feet.

Score: D   M   H/A

3. The finger looks like a seahorse.

(*Remind?*) It's a green seahorse.

Score: dr   FC   A   O

4. In the brown is a wolf's head with two little horns.

A horse's head and a wolf's head; just whatever you want.

Score: D   F   Ad

5. Looks like Teddy Roosevelt with a great big head and real little arms, sticking his tongue out.

Kinda like a little baby. It's really a baby, like in satirical cartoons, with big heads. The body is inconsequential.

Score: D   M   (Hd)

6. On the other side is a big head with a littler body, sticking out his tongue.

This is a bigger head. Just an old man with a moustache, sticking out his tongue.

Score: D   M   Hd

CARD X (3'') (Initial time 3'', total time 2' 42'')

This is a maze! Just a mess!

1. Here's a rabbit. And from his eyes, there's a moustache with two crossbars at the end.

Funny thing for a moustache to be growing out of its eyes, isn't it?

Score: D   F   Ad   P add. O-

2. The head of a horse but the body of a crab with the pincers sticking out.

Looks like it's mean. By the pupil of the eye, it looks like he's growling. The nose is partly covered by the pincers. By the way, this thing has a tail sticking up like a scorpion.

Score: D,S   F>M   (A)   add. P, O-

3. And one of the pincer's got a sheep-like thing.

> It's hard to find. Here's the sheep's head and a single horn like a unicorn. It's springing, like in mid-air.

Score: D   FM   A

4. And this long narrow body is like a baby with lips pouted and a curled nose.

> The turned nose makes me think of a baby pouting. Kind of like an embryo. Just the face and the rounded outline looks like an embryo.

Score: D   M   H

5. Three golden balls.

> Like the seal of Manucci family. What does that stand for? A jewelry or watch shop?

Score: D   FC   Emb.

6. Two animals and a tail on the long, narrow body of a child.

> A big eye, just a big eye. Not much to him, only one leg. (*Kind?*) I never saw an animal with one leg before. I wouldn't know what kind. (*Help?*) Any color, it's just because of the outline.

Score: D   F   A   O

7. Two seahorses' heads. Looks like they're pouting. Looks like they're on grain, a piece of grain.

> Pouting to a piece of grain, like some sort of sugared cereal. They blow them up and still they're the same size, puffed grain. They're like chesspieces, the horses' head. They don't eat grain. If you consider them people, then I think of human food rather than grain, but these aren't people, that's why it must be grain they're eating.

Score: D   FM>M   Ad

8. There's a pole in the background.

> (*Background?*) Yes, there are two heads overlapping the pole. They got five feelers, like little frogs with sheep's legs and tail, an eye like a cat with a vertical pupil. Looks like they're angry, talking to each other, facing each other. (*Other than shape?*) Color doesn't mean a thing to me.

Score: D   -   F,FK   obj/(A)

9. Some sort of another little crab.

> It could have its legs knocked off. A round old flat body and pinchers sticking around the side.

Score: D   F   A

TESTING THE LIMITS

Card I: (*Sometimes a winged animal like a butterfly or bat is seen on this* card. *Can you find it?*) "No." (*Holding the card this way, can you see it?*) "No." (Winged animal is pointed out.) "Yes, that could look like a bat."

Card IV: (*Sometimes a fur rug is seen here. Can you see it?*) "I can see a boot but I can't see any fur because of the coloring. Doesn't look like it to me."

Card VI: (*Sometimes a fur rug is seen here, too. Can you see it?*) "It could be." (Outlines with finger.) "But it looks more like a reptile skin; it has a slimy look. Definitely not fur; it makes me think of slime."

Card X: (*Sometimes this is seen as a tomato worm or a caterpillar because of both the elongated shape and the green coloring.*) "No, the end curls. It could look like an eel because of the dent at the neck. Caterpillars have segmentations. It's not the color. May be a garter snake, but not really."

Piles: "I'd group them mostly by color. The lighter greys"; (cards I and VII) "the red and dark black"; (cards II and III) "the darker blacks"; (cards IV and V). "This is just a light grey" (card VI) and could go with these (cards I and VII). "These are kind of sloppy; the color drips" (VIII and IX). "This one has clear outlines all the way, so it's in a separate class" (card X).

Like: (Card III) "The nice sharp outlines and the red and black. I didn't like this" (card II) "because it's smeary."

Dislike: (Card X) "Such a jumble. It's not pretty especially these" (lower red brown D).

The Rorschach, more than any other test, reveals the pathological extent of this boy's difficulties. The peculiar combination of meticulousness in detail and inappropriateness in generalization, manifested by well-specified details absurdly organized, is clearly analogous to schizophrenic thinking.

His thinking as revealed in the Rorschach is rigid and inflexible as brought out by his high $F\%$, without accompanying shock-absorbing factors. The relationship of parts and wholes in his content reveals the overcritical nature of his thinking. At the same time his superior endowment is clearly in evidence. His high ratio of responses to the colored cards when opposed to his few responses using color indicates the basic responsiveness of this boy to emotional situations, which, in this case is unaccompanied by any ability to handle these adequately. He appears to be extremely sensitive, but his inability to use this sensitivity to any constructive purpose in his interpersonal

RORSCHACH RECORD – Location Chart   Case of Mike ...

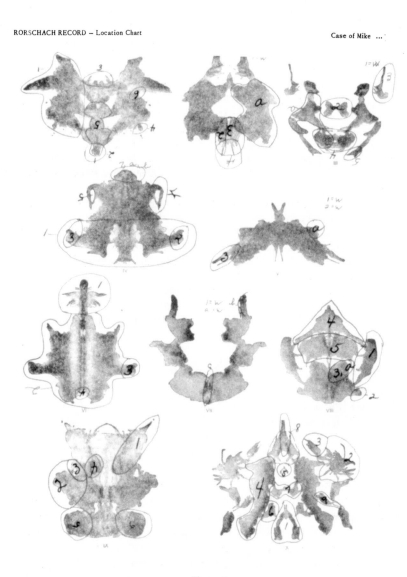

Figure 2

Rorschach Location Chart

relationships is demonstrated by his few *Fc* responses. His *M:Sum C* ratio is so loaded on the movement side that it must be interpreted as a morbid preoccupation with his own feelings and ideas. His confusion in regard to his own sexual role is demonstrated by his inability to identify the sex of the human figures perceived. The fact that he is extremely dependent is demonstrated by the many responses of open hands reaching out scattered throughout the record. What he considers animal-like tendencies were regarded with disdain, as in the "contented cow" response.

The boy's relative insensitivity to the needs of other people and the strained and artificial nature of his social relationships are demonstrated by the shading and color dynamics, respectively. The fact that he is critical of others is demonstrated by the relationship of parts to wholes, and his ethnic prejudices pervade the record. There are references throughout to human beings like Jews, Negroes or apes, with little distinction being made between these categories. The unpleasant affect associated with many of the human figures on the record demonstrates this boy's unhappy relationship with the world. More specifically, there are indications of resentment towards child rivals demonstrated by the many unpleasant remarks made about babies. Negative affect is demonstrated towards women, such as in the sarcastic response to card VII followed by the rather sadistic concept of a fly with its wings torn off.

There is some minimal awareness of his inner conflicts as shown by the *m* responses. However, the picture is basically that of an extremely schizoid individual as shown by the high number of fantasy figures, the jaundiced view of the world, the inability to deal with reality effectively, and the unevenness of intellectual performance. From the Rorschach one can only conclude that this boy is very close to an actual psychotic withdrawal of the paranoid sort.

Analysis of Bender-Gestalt Test

Mike was given the Bender twice. The first in the usual way, the second one with the added instruction of doing the job as quickly as possible. His first administration was finished in six minutes and eleven seconds and his second in three min-

RORSCHACH RECORD – Psychogram   Case of Mike ...

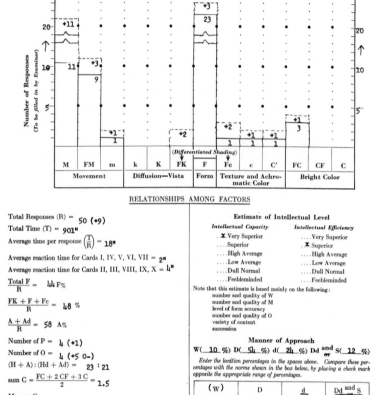

RELATIONSHIPS AMONG FACTORS

Total Responses (R) = **50 (+9)**

Total Time (T) = **901"**

Average time per response $\left(\frac{T}{R}\right)$ = **18"**

Average reaction time for Cards I, IV, V, VI, VII = **2"**

Average reaction time for Cards II, III, VIII, IX, X = **4"**

$\frac{\text{Total F}}{R}$ = **44** F%

$\frac{FK + F + Fc}{R}$ = **48** %

$\frac{A + Ad}{R}$ = **58** A%

Number of P = **4 (+1)**

Number of O = **4 (+5 0-)**

(H + A) : (Hd + Ad) = **23 : 21**

sum C = $\frac{FC + 2\ CF + 3\ C}{2}$ = **1.5**

M : sum C = **11 : 1.5**

(FM + m) : (Fc + c + C') = **10 : 3**

$\frac{\text{No. of responses to Cards VIII, IX, X}}{R}$ = **40** %

W : M = **5 : 11**

Succession :

Rigid   Orderly   Loose   Confused

(Place a check mark at the appropriate point on the scale above)

Estimate of Intellectual Level

Intellectual Capacity	*Intellectual Efficiency*
.**X** Very Superior	....Very Superior
....Superior	.**X** Superior
....High Average	....High Average
....Low Average	....Low Average
....Dull Normal	....Dull Normal
....Feebleminded	....Feebleminded

Note that this estimate is based mainly on the following :
number and quality of W
number and quality of M
level of form accuracy
number and quality of O
variety of content
succession

Manner of Approach

W(__10__%) D(__54__%) d(__24__%) Dd and S(__12__%)
                                      or

Enter the location percentages in the spaces above. Compare these percentages with the norms shown in the box below, by placing a check mark opposite the appropriate range of percentages.

(W)	D	d	Dd and or S
< 10% ((W))	< 30% ((D))		
10–20 (W)	30–45 (D)	< 5% (d)	
20–30 W	45–55 D	5–15 d	< 10% Dd S
30–45 W	55–65 D	15–25 d	10–15 Dd S
45–60 W	65–80 D	25–35 d	15–20 Dd S
> 60 W	> 80 D	35–45 d	20–25 Dd S
		> 45 d	> 25 Dd S

Figure 3

Rorschach Psychogram

utes and thirty-one seconds. Whenever the symbolic value of the figures is referred to below, it is based upon the article by Suczek and Klopfer (22).

On both administrations Mike put each of the figures on a separate page, usually exaggerating their size. His performance was expansive, but yet perfectionistic. In organizing the material in this way, he avoided the necessity for arranging the figures on a page, thus making it unnecessary to plan ahead or organize his material. In the first administration, he demonstrated emotional instability by the loss of angulation and other sloppy kinds of behavior which do not jibe with his intelligence. Inadequate reality ties were demonstrated by the distortion of the Gestalt of figure 3, in spite of the meticulous counting of the individual parts. Also, there was considerable overlap of the two parts of figure 1. Specific difficulty in the masculine role is demonstrated by the boy's inability to reproduce the upper elongated portion of figure 5 and the necessity of drawing this figure four times before he was satisfied with it.

The second administration of Bender is thought to arouse a conflict and put the patient under pressure. He reacted to this by a general improvement in the individual reproductions of the figures. He became increasingly expansive, but there was more compulsive counting behavior, and in general, they were reproduced more correctly. However, he did less well on that figure representing a complex situation (figure 7) than he did previously. Thus Mike may be said to improve under pressure, or perhaps as the result of practice, but appears to have specific difficulty in dealing with complex situations under such circumstances. This might represent some confusion in complex thinking under pressure.

Analysis of Drawings

In the absence of available standardized methods of analyzing drawings, the authors are presenting some of their hypotheses as is common in clinical practice.

The omission of legs in the female figure, the unattractive face, as well as Mike's derogatory comments accompanying his drawings, certainly suggest hostility. His near forgetting of her arms and their inclusion at the very end seems to suggest

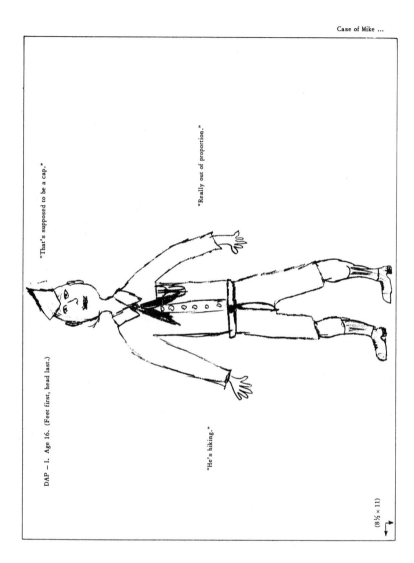

Figure 4

Drawing of Male

Figure 5

Drawing of Female

rejection of one of the bases of this hostility towards women. That some of his hostility may be directed specifically towards his mother is suggested by the extremely older appearance of the female than the male figure, despite Mike's stated ages of 16 and 20 years respectively. The extreme midline emphasis, collar, bow tie, buttons down the front, the pockets and belt on the male figure as well as the shading and neck ornamentation on the female figure may imply overt dependence.

Mike's drawing of the male figure reflects his desire to belong to a regimented society as revealed by the uniform in which this figure is clothed. The fact that the figure was drawn in sketchy lines and that Mike erased might reflect feelings of inadequacy and anxiety. The delineation of the crotch area might indicate that Mike has difficulties in the area of sexuality.

Test Integration

This patient has a superior intellectual potential which he can express only on a verbal level.

This is demonstrated by the Verbal-Performance discrepancy in the Wechsler-Bellevue. To some extent the better achievement in the Vigotsky as opposed to the Proverbs seems incongruous, but is rationalized on the basis of his greater efficiency in an impersonal task. His good verbal ability is also evident in both the case history and his behavior during the psychological examination.

He demonstrates exceptional ability to think along abstract lines and to form original ideas. However, he frequently puts a great deal of his intellectual energy into solving the most trivial problems. On the one hand, he becomes so immersed in the pseudotheoretical aspects of a problem that he misses the obvious. Yet, on the other hand, he may overelaborate the obvious with little realization of its essential triteness.

His lack of practical ability is demonstrated in the Wechsler. His verbalizations on the same test certainly tend to give an ostentatious impression. In the Picture Frustration Test he shows a tendency to gloss over situations and in the Bender-Gestalt he characteristically avoids organizing materials. How his attempts at abstraction go awry is seen in his Proverbs' performance and in the Rorschach protocol, in both of which his inappropriate use of organizational energy and his excessive meticulousness are clearly manifested.

Such poor judgment and lack of critical sense suggests that his ties to reality can waver considerably, as reflected in his reduced ability to meet practical problems. Despite a wide range of interests, he tends to theorize about the concrete rather than act upon his knowledge. Because of this lack of tangible experience, his theories and abstractions, while reflecting his potentialities for creative endeavor, are empty. He rarely allows this abstract matrix to be filled by solid, everyday experiences; instead, it remains a protective shell which shields him from awareness of frustrating reality.

His tendency to intellectualize is, of course, apparent throughout. His performance in the Picture Frustration Test suggests that his theoretical way of coping with frustrating situations is quite at variance with his actual behavior inferred from the other tests. In the MAPS he indicates that rational behavior is associated with masculinity, but also demonstrates his vague ties to reality. The Draw-A-Person Test reflects his desire to be dependent and to have a high degree of structure. Disturbances in formal thinking displayed in the Rorschach and Proverbs have certainly reduced his efficiency throughout. Very crucial evidence of this is his over-all inefficiency in life situations in contrast to his intellectual potential. With the number of prejudices and the poor social techniques that he has demonstrated, everyday interpersonal experiences cannot be anything but frustrating to him.

However, despite his emotional deprivation and the cultural abandonment he feels so keenly, reality is still quite attractive to him, and his resort to fantasy and abstraction is not very satisfying. He wants to relate in a mature way to other people and occasionally succeeds in being accepted by them.

His desire to be conventional is demonstrated by the Picture Frustration study and MMPI as well as by the Blacky Test. If he could only be accepted as a "good" boy and not have any demands made upon him, he feels that he would have no difficulty. It is only (*sic*) an insensitivity to others, coupled with a morbid preoccupation with himself, as demonstrated on the Rorschach, that prevents this happy state of affairs.

However, relating to people as in the intellectual sphere, he wavers in expressing his potential. He tries so hard to express himself emotionally that his affect becomes inappropriate, absurd and shallow. He has a conception of expected social and emotional reactions, but he has difficulty in expressing himself spontaneously. Basically he is a boy who goes to the party but sits in a corner all evening. He is emotionally stimulated, but has difficulty in expressing himself in the emotional sphere. As a last resort he capitalizes on his intellectual superiority to a pathologic degree.

Throughout there is a coupling of peculiar thinking with an indication of low subjective anxiety. The more structured the tasks (Wechsler, MMPI, Picture Frustration, Vigotsky), the more easily he is able to demonstrate adequate controls. With increasing ambiguity of the stimuli to which he is exposed, the pathology becomes more manifest. His performance in the Bender demonstrates emotional instability which is nonetheless reduced by increased structure. On the Sentence-Completion Test he seems to indicate a basic desire to be passive, as when exposed to adequately-authoritative situations. In the Rorschach, in spite of all the indications of rigid thinking in his attempts to withdraw from emotionally provoking situations, he nevertheless manifests a basic reactivity to complex emotional stimuli. In both the Blacky and the MMPI basic phobic material emerges despite all defensive maneuvers.

The reason for this affective inadequacy lies in his basically disparaging view of himself. Actually he is an extremely dependent boy whose need for love and respect has never been met. He keenly senses that his main prop of intellectual aspiration is very much at odds with the cultural barrenness of his family life. Since his roots are weak, he lacks the emotional integration to deal effectively with his disappointments.

His preoccupation with ethnic prejudices on the Rorschach as well as in his test behavior and history, clearly indicate uncertainty as to where he belongs. The MAPS test gives evidence to indicate that neither men nor women seem to him to be either effective or trustworthy, a view-point which can be gauged equally well from the Sentence-Completion Test and the Rorschach. In the test behavior he also bursts into tears after revealing so much uncertainty to himself and the examiner.

Instead he denies his hostility completely and puts up a front of amiability and passivity. His is a veneer of logic and reason behind which emotions must be inhibited for the greater good. The need to create such a veneer of extreme rationality gives some clue to the intensity of the emotions which it keeps in check.

The Blacky Test indicates strong defenses of denial, repression and intellectualization. The Rorschach gives the impression of one who is unable to deal with reality effectively, but must use projection and escape into fantasy as a substitute. The blocking of associative thinking in the Sentence-Completion, together with the generally non-committal nature of his responses, yield further clues to the intensity of the denial process. In both the MMPI and the Picture Frustration Test the veneer is much more in evidence than is the underlying feeling.

Although he can only express his aggression verbally, his needs for succorance are so great and the possibility of satisfying them seems so hopeless to him that he refuses to accept himself on other than an intellectual basis. He deprecates himself for the intensity of his needs and hates other people for never having satisfied them. Since his severe dependency interferes with his rational self-concept, he projects these unacceptable feelings on others.

His dependency needs break through in the Blacky Test and in the DAP, although they are generally kept fairly well hidden. His tendency to project onto others his own sense of inadequacy is most obvious in the extreme hostility evident in the history, test behavior, Rorschach, Sentence-Completion Test, Proverbs, and, to some extent, the MMPI.

Other people comprise emotional, impulsive, irrational, infantile hordes, while he is the logician who can put his intellectual gifts to work. Thus, presently a dichotomy of good and evil is in the process of being established, good symbolizes the calm, thinking philosopher, evil the primitive emotions.

Good and evil are most clearly dichotomized on the

MAPS, but are implied throughout by his ambivalence about whether to conform or rebel. It is difficult to know from his Sentence-Completion items whether his desire to rebel or his desire to submit is the more ego-syntonic. Certainly one gets the impression from the Wechsler-Bellevue that an intellectual level of aspiration is considered a most adequate defense against feelings of insecurity and inadequacy. The history indicates that intellectual endeavor has always been his favorite technique for quelling emotional upsets.

With his fear of emotionality, it follows that sexuality has also been removed from his consciousness because of its primitive nature. His own sexual role is not definite—again he wavers between the extremes of masculinity and femininity. On the one hand, he would like to identify with an all-powerful, physically able, punitive father figure, but he cannot meet the emotional challenge of such perfect status. On the other hand, he prefers the advantages of femininity where his passivity would be acceptable and where he could compete adequately with his sister for his parent's affection. Thus, again he leans heavily on his intellect to compromise with his sexual conflict and becomes the coolheaded, desexualized philosopher possessed with masculine reason and feminine passivity.

It is evident from the Sentence-Completion Test that although he experiences stronger subjective ambivalence toward men, women are very mysterious and disturbing. His desire to submit to regimentation, as demonstrated on the DAP, dovetails with his attempt to give the impression of a conventionally-submissive individual in the Picture-Frustration study. However, he demonstrates much sexual confusion in the Blacky, with the implication that being a woman is certainly easier than being a man. Indications of sibling rivalry in the Rorschach and Blacky may indicate that the sex of the successful sibling (female) might have confused his goals in this regard.

His defenses of repression, overintellectualization, and compulsiveness have not alleviated his severe anxiety. Inasmuch as his anxiety-tolerance is low, he retreats into fantasies of himself as master of all situations (but actually master of his emotions), receiving love and admiration from everyone as compensation for what he has never felt in reality. He is still checking reality, nevertheless, because of the possibility that it may meet his needs. When his own needs and the frustrations in his world become so anxiety-provoking that intellectualization does not work, he retreats into fantasy, an exaggeration of his intellectual defenses. His resort to fantasy and his surrender of reality ties are currently becoming more severe.

The more intellectual and less pathological defenses are evident in almost every stimulus situation to which he has been exposed. He shows intellectualizing tendencies in the Wechsler, defensive behavior in the MMPI, a tendency to use intellectualization as a defense against ego-alien impulses in the MAPS, rigid and overcritical thinking in the Rorschach, and all of these in the Blacky Test. His more pathologic techniques of reducing anxiety are observable on a gradient from the Rorschach at the one extreme to the Vigotsky at the other. Disturbances in formal thinking that might be considered schizophrenic occur in the Wechsler, MAPS, Proverbs, Sentence-Completion Test, and Rorschach. In addition, the Rorschach, MMPI, and Sentence-Completion Test tend to give the picture of a rather schizoid view of life. This is evident in his discernible proneness to retreat to fantasy and isolate the affect usually associated with interpersonal situations.

Prognosis

For maximum benefit from psychotherapy, he must be provided with an extremely warm, accepting relationship. He will probably test out the therapist repeatedly so as to assure himself that he is truly understood and respected. While intellectualizing with the patient is to be avoided, this neurotic prop must initially be accepted. As he finds satisfaction in the therapeutic relationship, particularly with a man with whom he can identify, he can slowly surrender his resort to fantasy and, finally, his intellectual defenses.

Summary

This is an extremely bright boy who can express his potential only on a verbal, abstract level. His capacity for dealing with practicalities has been considerably diminished since he has rarely allowed himself to make sufficient contact with concrete, mundane aspects of reality. He is extremely sensitive to his lack of physical prowess, which represents strength and manhood to him. His role in the family was undermined by a younger sister who seems to get the love and attention from the parents which he craves. He grew up in a sterile cultural atmosphere which was at great odds with his own cultural aspirations. He capitalized on the one sphere in which he felt superior to others—the intellect.

His own needs had to be subordinated because they were so intense and because the possibility of satisfying them seemed hopeless. To him emotions are synonomous with impulsiveness, dependency, the irrational, and most of all, femininity; these qualities reflect one aspect of himself, which he must repress. He feels the intellect to be synonomous with reason, mastery, independence, and most of all, masculinity. He can accept himself in this role. Thus he has a tendency to dichotomize the ideational and affective. However, some of his emotional needs are sufficiently conscious to cause him considerable anxiety which is partially absorbed by neurotic defenses. However, because of the inadequacy of this intellectual defense and because his anxiety tolerance is low, this patient often resorts to psychotic mechanisms of autism and projection. This is a patient with a basically schizoid personality, who comes very close to paranoid schizophrenia at the present time.

APPENDIX

Illustrative Reports

THIS APPENDIX contains sample psychological reports of the author. They represent a variety of problems and styles and should be evaluated by the reader in the light of the suggestions made in the preceding sections.

I.

This is the report of the psychological evaluation of a nine-year-old boy. It demonstrates the use of test data for illustrative purposes when the report is given in an interdisciplinary setting.

As is typical in many such child cases, this report makes frequent reference to the relationship of present functioning to developmental level. An attempt is made to distinguish between psychological phenomena occurring at different personality levels: public, conscious and private. At the end of the report the basic symptom causing the referral is discussed in the light of the psychological findings.

Referred By

Out-patient clinic for aid in diagnostic evaluation and treatment planning.

Tests Administered

  Stanford-Binet Vocabulary
  Children's Sentence-Completion Test
  Draw-A-Person
  Children's Apperception Test
  Rorschach
  Roger's Personality Adjustment Test

Behavior During Examination

Jack was polite and cooperative during the examination. Only at first did he seem rather defensive and self-critical, being somewhat bothered when he was unable to respond appropriately to a question. He worked rapidly and efficiently and showed no demonstrable anxiety or fear in the situation.

Analysis of Test Data

Jack is a boy of average intelligence who seemingly has had no difficulty accomplishing what might be ordinarily expected at his age. He described himself as doing very inadequate school work, referring to a *B* average with grades between *A* and *C*. Such self-criticism probably reflects excessive aspirations on the part of the parents. He does especially well in tasks requiring concentration and makes concerted efforts for brief periods of time. However, his attention span is limited and, like other boys of his age, he soon tends to lose interest. He is able to understand the rules of society reasonably well and can accept most conventional lines of thinking except those pertaining to interpersonal relationships, but he does not seem to feel close to other people and has little understanding of the mechanics of affective interaction. As emotional stresses and strains mount, his ability to exert rational control over his behavior diminishes.

This boy's self-concept is very unusual for his age. He feels inadequate in almost every area of life. He would like to be the reverse of what he is and is completely unable to say anything favorable about himself. He feels torn by inconsistent needs, bothered by guilt, and is extremely self-punitive. He feels lacking in the social graces and has much resentment simmering close to the surface, but not currently being admitted. He feels that society has rejected him and that the future holds little immediate hope since the world seems to him a rather savage place. He tends occasionally to be critical of others and puts on a bold front, but basically he is more critical toward himself.

An outstanding finding was the extreme hostility this boy demonstrated toward women, apparently deriving from his relationship with his mother. He obviously prefers the father. (On the Rorschach he sees a pig wearing a dress, a girl with poison spiders crawling over her, and throughout the self-administered tests he consistently demonstrates preference for the father.)

Impressions

On the basis of the psychological tests administered, Jack's presenting symptom of petty thievery can best be understood as being motivated by a combination of a desire for affection which has been withheld and retaliation or hostility against society. He is very self-critical and demonstrates a desire to change. He is interested in improving his relationship with his parents, but particularly with his playmates. He seems to want more structure and feels that the rules of society have not been made sufficiently explicit for him. He sees little happiness in childhood and dreams of the future when he might be happier. Depending on the attitude of the parents, this child could well be considered a candidate for psychotherapy in a play setting.

2.

This report of a 16-year-old boy was prepared at the request of a State Department of Vocational Rehabilitation. Its brevity is consistent with the sparsity of available data. The emphasis here is on existent and potential areas of efficiency and inefficiency in situations typical of potential work placements. The boy's strengths and weaknesses have been gauged in line with possible recommendations to counselors and potential employers.

Referred By
Department of Vocational Rehabilitation for intellectual and diagnostic evaluation.

Tests Administered
Rorschach
Wechsler-Bellevue, Form I

Behavior During Examination
The patient said he was somewhat nervous at the outset, but showed no signs of discomfort during subsequent evaluation. In fact, his affect appeared quite flat. He readily complied with all that was asked of him and did not directly seek reassurance.

Analysis of Test Data
Intellectual evaluation indicated that this patient is of average ability. His performance was quite spotty, inconsistent, and occasionally sloppy and haphazard. He tends to do considerably better on motor tasks than on verbal ones; he seems handicapped in his verbal thought processes by rather marked preoccupations with his own problems, preventing him from attending to the task at hand.

Emotionally, he is very much afraid of the world, frightened of the people in it, and tends to withdraw and shut himself in. He probably daydreams a great deal, since fantasy seems much more attractive to him than reality which has apparently been a source of considerable unhappiness. Subjectively he feels very inadequate and appears to feel that he is being too closely observed and supervised by other people.

Diagnostic Impression
This boy's perceptions are quite vague and often approach the bizarre. His affect is rather flat and withdrawn and his interets in further maturation seems minimal at this time. Although this examiner is very hesitant to suggest such a diagnosis in the case of a 16-year-old boy, the psychological data point to the presence of a schizophrenic

condition. The results of this examination will be taken together with a social history gathered by the social worker and recommendations will be made to Vocational Rehabilitation.

3.

This is an evaluation of a 15-year-old boy, the product of a broken home. Despite this boy's severe environmental deprivations the report emphasizes his many personality assets, thereby contrasting with reports in which generally well-adjusted people with manifold ego-resources are too often described only in terms of their shortcomings. The report also sharply distinguishes between events going on within the boy's fantasy and his public effectiveness in everyday situations.

It should be noted that this report, like some of the others, does not contain a behavioral note. On the basis of experiences in recent years, I have become convinced that the behavioral observations are an important part of the psychological evaluation and should be seriously considered in any conclusions or recommendations that are made.

Referral
    For prognostic evaluation.
Tests Administered
    Rorschach
    TAT
    Wechsler-Bellevue, Form I (in part)
    Sentence Completion Test
    Draw-A-Person
Analysis of Data
    Frank's performance on the psychological tests shows him to be of considerably above average intelligence. He has good ties to reality and is well able to appreciate conventional lines of thinking and behavior. He is able to succeed in practical tasks, engage in abstract thinking requiring planning ahead, and manage other problems of an intellectual nature.

    The patient has a rich fantasy life and good imagination which could ultimately be used for creative or constructive purposes. At present his fantasy life serves mainly as a depository for his many feelings of frustration and hostility which do not find adequate outward expression. He is extremely sensitive, and is easily upset and frustrated by things happening around him. Potentially he is a very warm, emotionally-alive person, but currently appears rather withdrawn. His self-concept, characteristic of his age group, is extremely mixed-up. He is extremely self-conscious, readily accusing himself of innumerable misdemeanors about which he feels guilty. He alternates between being rebellious and passive and is generally "in a stew." He has strong feelings of both warmth and hostility, neither of which finds adequate expression in his overt behavior. (One of the strongest feelings is that of conscious jealousy toward his sister's children, of which he is very much ashamed.)

The patient has good basic capacities for adjusting to the world and for relating to other people. Even at present his social technique is appropriate for a boy of his age. On the other hand, he conceives of an ideal mother-figure and an ideal father-figure, neither one of which might ever have existed in reality. His sister and brother-in-law, when compared to these ideal figures, turn out to be rather inadequate. He feels very rejected by them and often regards them as treating him unfairly. Women appear to him as rather dominant figures who seem to control men; however, his relationships with men appear to be somewhat smoother and more tranquil than those with women.

At the present time this boy is very mixed-up. He is venting feelings of frustration derived from the home on his school work, in spite of the fact that he would really like to do well in school. He runs away because he feels rejected, only to feel even more rejected. Many of his fantasies have the flavor of "when I am gone, then they'll be sorry." In addition, there are possible complicating factors which may be related to the attitude of his sister and brother-in-law. These individuals will be seen shortly and a comprehensive evaluation of the case made at that time.

4.

Next is the report of the psychological examination of an adult mental defective. The behavioral note deals with the individual's reaction to a known symptom, his intellectual inadequacy. Contrary to usual practice, the IQ is reported simply because listing such a score is a legal necessity for a diagnosis of mental retardation. In the discussion of the patient's intellectual strengths and weaknesses, the emphasis is on the relative amount of retardation in various kinds of functioning tapped by the test battery. Even though the initial focus is on the intellectual problems of the individual, it is made clear that he does have personality problems which are then introduced into the report, an all too infrequent practice with patients of this kind.

Referred By

Physician for psychological examination.

Tests Administered

Rorschach
Bender-Gestalt
Wechsler-Bellevue, Form I

Behavior

The patient was rather nervous and afraid at the beginning of the psychological examination. His hands shook and he perspired freely, although shortly after he became accustomed to the situation this behavior disappeared. Much of the time he was preoccupied with his present commitment, wanted to go fishing and engage in other activities, and would every once in a while interrupt his test performance to ask the examiner about his future.

Analysis of Test Data

Psychological tests administered to this patient make it evident that he is severely mentally retarded. (His Full Scale IQ on the Wechsler-Bellevue was 56.) His performance was consistently very inadequate. His fund of general information, his judgment in social situations, and his ability to plan ahead are all severely retarded. He seems to do a trifle better in simple tasks requiring elementary hand-eye coordination, but even here his ability is quite limited. He is unable to plan ahead adequately, his perception of the world around him is very vague, his thinking is disjointed and fragmented, and his ability to sustain attention for any length of time is very limited.

The picture is that of a sensitive, rather cyclothymic kind of personality who, because of his severe sense of inferiority and inadequacy, easily has his feelings hurt, but just as easily overcomes this feeling. (Typical of his behavior is his Rorschach performance: "A butterfly" on the first card seemed to him an adequate way of handling the situation, with the result that he gave exactly the same response to each of the nine succeeding cards. When requested to go through the cards again and see something other than butterflies, he simply perseverated with a new response throughout.) This exemplifies the kind of "magic perseveration" used by very young children for mastering an environment that seems overwhelming and threatening to them; they use previously successful mechanisms of adaption in situations where these are now completely inappropriate.

It is most difficult on the basis of psychological tests to evaluate the reality ties of this individual. A person as severely retarded as this patient naturally does not have adequate ties to reality. The point at which this condition could be termed a mental deficiency with psychotic reaction is difficult to determine. The fact is that the psychological tests do not present any direct evidence of psychosis in addition to mental deficiency. Instead, the results would be most in line with a diagnosis of mental deficiency, severe, with behavioral reaction.

5.

The following report describes a young woman who was evaluated as a candidate for out-patient therapy. The psychiatrist who uses an analytically-oriented form of treatment is interested in a detailed discussion about the patient's dynamics, especially from a prognostic viewpoint. In the report there is an attempted unravelling of layers of defense down to the basic conflicts and their etiology. A thorough attempt was made to evaluate the patient's motivation for change. It seems less hazardous to speculate in the case of an individual about to enter psychotherapy since any interpretations deviating radically from the truth will be uncovered during the course of further contacts.

Referred By

Psychiatrist for personality evaluation.

Tests Administered

Rorschach
TAT

Analysis of Data

This patient seems to have about average intellectual potential. At present she is functioning below this level because much of her energy is taken up by an effort to deal with her severe emotional difficulties. Her preoccupations with her problems cause her thinking to be stereotyped and trite. She prefers handling situations piece-meal to avoid the confusion caused by complexities.

She is very much disturbed by any emotional situation. She has a feeling that she is helpless to handle such situations in any reasonable or constructive fashion. Emotion, in her mind, seems to be equated with unbridled sensuality and this prospect frightens her very much. She seems to be basically a very erotic, passionate person, who has learned to hide and inhibit these characteristics from other people and herself. Emotional stimulation, in her mind, seems to lead to erotic behavior, which in turn is closely allied with conception. For her, conception is a very painful process and even the pleasure of love seems hardly worth such a dismal end. She is extremely indecisive. Her mixed feelings on various subjects make any decision virtually impossible for her. Although she tends to have some fantasy life, her fantasy gives little satisfaction because of the constant intrusion of reality problems. She is deeply ashamed of her inadequacies and would like to hide them from others if this were only possible.

She wants very badly to get along with others, to love and be loved. She tries to meet every social situation in the best way she can. However, much of her behavior is stereotyped and not necessarily appropriate to the specific demands of the situation in which she finds herself. People are very difficult for her to deal with. She tends to idealize them and consequently finds real people rather disappointing. The fact that she wants people to be perfect makes it difficult for her to accept them as she actually finds them in everyday life. In addition, she is rather suspicious of others and tends to attribute somewhat more maliciousness to them than is reasonable.

A good part of her problem seems to be a feeling of guilt stemming from her repressed erotic desires. She is afraid of men because she is really afraid of herself. She tends to reject them because of her own fear of being rejected by them for her unworthiness.

Her feelings about women also constitute a major problem. She apparently feels very rejected by her mother. (Her mother appears in her fantasy production as a cold, frigid and unapproachable person.) Even her fiancé's mother crops up as a competitor. She also expresses very strong feelings about her sister and other female contemporaries. These feelings of bitterness and hate are not consciously acceptable to the patient because they are quite incompatible with her accepted code of morals and the teachings of her church. Yet, these thoughts of hate continue to gnaw at her vitals.

Although the patient tries desperately to evade the problems which are constantly coming up, anxiety continues to break through to a considerable degree. She apparently feels confused and inadequate. She is afraid of the future and feels quite unhappy and depressed at times. Yet, the examiner feels that the patient has fair potentialities for adjustment because of her sincere interest in wanting to get along with people and the fact that her instinctual feelings are not very deeply repressed.

The diagnosis of anxiety state proposed seems a good description of this patient.

6.

This report illustrates the evaluation of an elderly lady. The patient, age 77, was evaluated to see whether hospitalization was necessary or whether out-patient treatment could be recommended as an alternative. Here again the patient's personality assets are discussed in some detail. An attempt is made to evaluate her adjustment outside of an institution and to discover the secondary gains associated with her symptoms. The report concludes with a specific recommendation as to hospitalization *on the basis of psychological test data.* The final decision, of course, should be made on the basis of all available sources of information.

Referred By

Psychiatrist for diagnostic evaluation.

Tests Administered

Bender-Gestalt
Rorschach
Benjamin's Proverbs

Analysis of Data

The picture is that of a very bright, very imaginative old lady with a rich fantasy life who is functioning at a high peak of intellectual efficiency for her age. She is not exceptionally ambitious in the intellectual sphere, but is easy going and relaxed. She is well able to handle the details of everyday life, and to obtain some perspective and evaluate the over-all aspects of a situation. She can easily comprehend conventional ideas and formulate unusual and original ones of her own. There also are some indications that she may have considerable artistic and creative ability.

She has an essentially good opinion of herself and tries to do a competent job of whatever work happens to fall to her. She is self-critical and able to improve her performance when necessary. However, her self-concept is essentially the narcissistic one of a "delicate flower," and she becomes most upset when she fails to receive the attention and affection which she feels her due. Although she ordinarily has fairly satisfactory ways of relating to other people, she is essentially suspicious of them and easily becomes frustrated when insufficient attention is given her.

Although she occasionally rebels against authority, she seems to have no real desire for independence. Her ways of relating to men have apparently been less adequate than her relationships with women,

men being considered essentially clumsy brutes who are best avoided. She is sensitive and easily inclined to worry when something goes wrong. Her symptoms, whatever their origin, fulfill the secondary function of drawing attention to herself and gaining sympathy.

In conclusion, the picture is essentially that of a hysteroid personality—sensitive, dependent, essentially narcissistic, and with an insatiable need for attention from others. It is beyond the scope of this report to discuss the etiology of her symptoms, but there is no doubt that they serve a very definite function in the equilibrium of her personality. Before she can be induced to give up these symptoms, it will probably be necessary to give her enough attention through frequent interviews to replace whatever attention she seems to have missed as a result of recent circumstances in her life.

Analysis of the present data shows no evidence of psychotic thinking or personality disintegration. The patient's emotional difficulties do not appear to be sufficiently severe to warrant hospitalization at the present time on those grounds.

7.

This report presents the psychological evaluation of a student at the request of a college dean. It should be noted that if the report were submitted to the dean as it stands, it would be not only incomprehensible but very disturbing to him. Consequently, it is intended only for the clinic files. The report actually given to the dean was mainly oral and was phrased quite differently, although the conclusions and recommendations remained essentially the same. As stated in earlier sections psychological reports should not be made to serve too many purposes at once lest they serve none of them well.

Referral

This student was referred by the Dean of Teacher's College for psychological evaluation to assist in determining the nature and severity of her emotional problems and to help in planning her future.

Tests Administered

Rorschach
Bender-Gestalt
TAT
Wechsler-Bellevue, Form I
Sentence Completion Test

Behavior During Examination

The patient was polite and cooperative during the examination, readily complying with all that was asked of her. She appeared flushed and tense, but otherwise manifested little emotion during the session. However, at the conclusion of the session she did complain of becoming confused under stress.

Analysis of Test Data

Intellectually this patient shows gross impairment in virtually all areas. Her potentialities demonstrate themselves only in tasks in which she can draw on knowledge acquired over a long period of time. She does very simple tasks with speed and efficiency, but a sudden drop in performance manifests itself with the first appearance of complexity. She has considerable difficulty in understanding things the way most people do. Vague feelings of disorganization and confusion constantly beset her. She tends to interpret situations on the basis of very minimal evidence, with the result that her perceptions of the world are often faulty.

The patient's emotional life is exceedingly turbulent. Drives of all kinds find ready expression, with inhibitory factors being virtually absent. Whenever affect appears, reason seemingly goes out the window. The patient, basically of a very intense nature, has been exceedingly frustrated by society's inability or unwillingness to meet her needs. She is completely unable to judge her relationships with people with any degree of accuracy, since reality is so extremely unpleasant.

Although the patient verbalizes feelings of self-criticalness, she is making no effort at this time to modify her thinking or behavior. Rather, she is constantly attempting to escape from one stressful situation (often, in fact, to another), hoping that change will prove the panacea for her problems. Basically she would prefer marriage to any career, but feels herself inadequate for gaining this goal.

At present she bitterly resents society, on which she lays the blame for her frustration. Her ability to accept or identify with others is minimal, and teaching would not seem a very profitable career for her at this point. She does not feel close to her relatives, her community or, in fact, anyone. She seems particularly critical of men, implying that they have frustrated or disappointed her in some way.

Summary and Impressions

The patient's needs, both passive and aggressive, are finding ready expression owing to her complete lack of control. Her intellectual defenses are proving pitifully inadequate. Reality is simplified by her in line with her desires and insight seems completely lacking. Considerable help will have to be given this girl before she can reasonably contemplate any career.

8.

The following is the report of the psychological examination of a woman with a borderline psychotic condition. A detailed description of the behavior during the examination is included because it seems particularly crucial in this case. Some of the findings governing basic personality traits derived from the psychological tests seem divergent superficially, but are subsequently integrated into a total personality picture in which each source of information makes its unique contribution. Much attention is paid throughout to the necessity for distinguishing various levels of the personality.

Referral

Referred by family physician for aid in evaluation and possible treatment.

Tests Administered

Rorschach
Bender-Gestalt
Sentence Completion
MMPI (Incomplete)

Behavioral Observation

This patient was most dependent during the psychological examination. She requested water and Coca Cola, wanted to be asked the MMPI questions rather than sorting the cards herself, and continuously complained of language difficulties which were more apparent than real. She talked incessantly of various physical symptoms and finally had to terminate the examination because she did not feel well enough to continue. She said that she had no emotional problems, but just wanted someone to do something to her (*sic*) to make her well.

Analysis of Test Data

This patient seems to be potentially of about average intellectual ability, but is currently unable to use her resources effectively because of severe, incapacitating emotional problems. A situation of any complexity or one involving stress immobilizes her intellectual energies. Her ties to reality, although usually adequate, sometimes appear rather loose.

The patient is very inhibited emotionally, showing a kind of blandness sometimes referred to as "belle indifference." She is extremely suggestible and will go along with anything designed to please other people and to fit in with her needs. The only feeling she can express freely is that of dependency, which is expressed to the exclusion of everything else. Rejection of her dependency needs almost drives her frantic and produces a great exacerbation of affective symptoms. She is quite concerned about sex and privately feels quite erotically attracted to others; however, consciously she is very moralistic and considers all ideas of this kind as reprehensible and taboo. She sometimes fears becoming psychotic, which is expressed as a fear of "losing her mind." Her usual state is one of rejection and subjective feelings of insecurity and indecisiveness. However, she fails to recognize any of her emotions as problems and thinks of her condition as purely physical.

Her attitude toward others is basically quite disinterested because of her extreme narcissism. At the same time she is markedly immature and dependent and needs others around to meet her own needs, even though she can do nothing to meet theirs in return. When they fail to meet her insatiable needs for affection and attention she becomes very disgruntled and her symptoms are intensified.

Summary and Impressions

This is a patient who from time to time expresses some rather peculiar ideas. She feels that she can be cured of illness by some sort of magical means. She expresses the feeling that no one can be trusted and sometimes is quite inconsistent in her perception of reality. However, these symptoms which ordinarily might point to more severe pathology are greatly outweighed by the plethora of neurotic symptomatology. Her only consistent reaction to stress is somatization. This, coupled with her extreme immaturity and overdependency, gives a picture which can best be described as a conversion reaction.

This person seems an extremely poor risk for psychotherapy. There is probably little to be done for her in the out-patient clinic.

9.

This report illustrates a patient suffering from chronic brain syndrome associated with cerebral arteriosclerosis, whose psychological examination findings are described more in terms of pathology than personality. Again the behavior during the examination is described in detail and in this instance dovetails quite closely with the difficulties revealed by individual diagnostic tests. Even in the case of an obvious organic condition such as this, the further refinement of diagnosis as between a psychotic, neurotic or behavioral reaction is required.

Referral

Referred by physician for aid in diagnostic evaluation.

Tests Administered

Rorschach

Wechsler-Bellevue, Form I

Behavior During Examination

The patient was exceedingly dependent, querulous, and suspicious during the examination. She requested constant reassurance which, when given, was of no avail. She refused to accept the statement that there was no right or wrong answers on the Rorschach, and kept asking the examiner whether her responses were "correct." She was very slow in all that she did and expressed continuous feelings of inadequacy and impotence.

Analysis of Test Data

Intellectually the patient shows definite effects of deterioration. Her over-all functioning is currently at the dull normal level, even though she evidently had average ability at one time. The irregular pattern of her successes and failures demonstrates the presence of better ability residually. She finds it very difficult to concentrate, and a task of any complexity is completely beyond her. She is exceedingly self-critical and is constantly berating herself for her inadequacy.

Emotionally the patient has the alternative of being restricted in the expression of her feelings or developing a passive sort of panic reaction. Her social skills are badly impaired because of the loss of confidence in herself suffered as a result of the aging process. She attempts to use compulsive techniques in a vain effort to relieve anxiety. Most life situations at present tend to confuse and perplex her. She tries to get along by soliciting pity from others so that they will forgive her inadequacies.

Summary and Impressions

The data suggest a typically senile individual who shows intellectual deterioration, impotence, perplexity, and suspiciousness toward others. She is very self-effacing and self-critical and cannot deal with others very effectively. The diagnosis most in line with the psychological test findings is that of chronic brain syndrome on an arteriosclerotic basis. There is no evidence of a psychotic reaction, but rather the overlay approximates a neurotic one.

10.

This report is adapted to the needs of a physician in a state hospital who has had no particular training in psychiatry. The distinction to be made is that between paranoid schizophrenia and a paranoid personality. The report is intended to illustrate the use of basic English in communicating some rather complex concepts. For instance, the concept of "projection" is conveyed by the statement, "there is considerable tendency on his part to attribute to others feelings and ideas originally emanating from within himself and not at all appropriately aimed at these other people." Such translation of "dynamic" concepts into everyday language is in line with the terminology proposed.

Referred By
Physician for diagnostic evaluation.

Tests Administered
Rorschach
Rosenzweig PF Test
Sentence Completion Test
Bender-Gestalt
Wechsler-Bellevue, Form I

Analysis of Data
On the basis of his performance on the intelligence test, this patient seems to be of superior intelligence, with an IQ of 125 on the Wechsler Scale. He seems superior in almost every regard, being especially good at tasks involving close attention and concentration. Not only does he show the ability to handle practical tasks, but he is able to look at the over-all aspects of a situation and to engage in abstract thinking and other types of higher mental activity. Social judgment, as revealed by his verbalizations on this test, is also adequate.

Emotionally, the patient tends to be extremely cautious, reserved, and inhibited, at least in his nonalcoholic state. His superior intelligence permits him to dissemble the basically aggressive, hostile impulses the presence of which may be inferred from his overt behavior when under the influence of alcohol. His conscious self-concept is that of a "good fellow" who tries to do the right thing and get along with people as best he can. There is some evidence to indicate that he has considerable frustrated ambition and feels tied down and depressed by not having achieved any more in his life than he has. This frustration makes him moody, suspicious and inclined toward drink.

On the one hand, this patient considers it extremely important to be liked and appreciated. In his ordinary sober state he tries to play the role of a passive, submissive individual who will do anything for the sake of getting along with others. He becomes aggressive only when directly challenged. However, basically he is extremely sus-

picious of other people, resents those in authority, and feels that everyone is trying to dominate him. This feeling extends to his wife who,
from his viewpoint, is trying to dominate and run him. Needless to
say he resents this bitterly. Actually, he has derived very little satisfaction from relationships with those close to him.

There is a considerable tendency on his part to attribute to others
feelings and ideas originally emanating from within himself and not
at all appropriately aimed at these other people. His inner feelings of
insecurity make him feel that others think little of him and are trying
to do things to frustrate him. As a result, he is very suspicious and
angry with them. There are some hints in his performance on the psychological tests which indicate that he feels hospitalization is doing
him little good and that he may attempt to escape if this is possible.

In conclusion, there is ample evidence of this patient's paranoid
thinking and his personality inadequacies, but there is no evidence in
any of the psychological tests clearly establishing a basis for considering this patient as currently in a psychotic state. He shows no disorders
of thinking, no bizarre perceptions, no mental deterioration, or any
other symptoms which might point in that direction. However, since
this patient's superior intelligence enables him to cover up basic dis-
integrative tendencies in his personality more successfully than would
be possible for another kind of patient, further examination at a later
date would seem indicated.

II.

This report was prepared at the request of a psychiatrist
who was puzzled by the patient's inconsistent symptomatology,
which manifested both affective and schizophrenic elements.
As is so often the case, clinical symptoms here are paralleled by
psychological test data, to the confusion of the psychologist
also. The test results did not aid in clarifying the picture, a fact
which is admitted in the report. It is never justifiable to arbi-
trarily force data into a frame of reference simply for the sake
of making a decision which is otherwise difficult.

Referred By

Psychiatrist for aid in diagnostic evaluation. The patient seems to
show both symptoms of a schizophrenic and affective nature.

Tests Administered

Rorschach

Bender-Gestalt
Benjamin's Proverbs
MMPI

Behavior During Examination

The patient was polite and cooperative during the examination, readily complying with all instructions given insofar as his condition permitted. He was inconsistent in his ability to supply basic information and his affect was variable. During the early part of the examination he complained of "nervousness," but when seen in the afternoon of the same day he claimed to be feeling better.

Analysis of Test Data

The patient seems to function adequately in the intellectual area as long as he is able to deal with immediate highly-structured situations in which he can employ rote memory. However, his basic ability to accurately perceive the environment is sometimes very doubtful. He shows a pathologic inability to plan ahead, to generalize from the immediate, and to engage in abstract types of mental activity.

He shows a complete inability to react spontaneously to other people's feelings or to express in a normal way the drives which motivate his behavior. He makes a great point of denying the presence of hostility which nonetheless seems present in considerable amount. He also finds it very difficult to express affection or any positive feelings toward others, presenting a picture of gross inhibition of all affect. Whether this inhibition is of a conscious sort, or whether it is unconscious in the form of repression, is not fully clear.

It would seem that the patient had a high level of aspiration and that there must be considerable dissatisfaction about some of the lack of success in his past life. He seems to have an underlying feeling that society is to blame, although attempting to deny it at the present time. When he succeeds in blaming himself, a kind of dysphoric reaction is in evidence. Whether such reaction is of a transient nature or is a more permanent part of his personality is difficult to determine.

Summary and Impressions

Some of the test results seem to point to a basic pathology of a schizophrenic nature—his complete inability to express his feelings, his occasional tendency to wander away from the point, his idiosyncratic perceptions, and his tendency to overdeny and, occasionally, to project. It is likely that the chronic personality picture is characterized by compulsive behavior and a paranoid kind of suspiciousness of other people and their possible reactions. However, at the present time there are definite affective symptoms in evidence. These include sporadic outbursts of anxiety and a tendency towards self-blame and depression. The diagnostic description of this patient most congruent with the total test data is that of a chronically schizoid-paranoid personality who is presently demonstrating diffuse affective symptomatology of a transient nature.

12.

In any clinical setting many patients are evaluated who seem to conform to certain stereotypes. An example is the alcoholic who suffers from a character disorder of which his alcoholic indulgence is the major symptom. In many such instances both the psychiatric and psychological evaluations probably fall into a pattern. There seems little point in elaborating at great length in a case of this kind. Instead, a relatively brief report is more in accord with the minimal contribution to be made by the psychological examination to the understanding of such individuals.

Referred By
Physician for aid in diagnostic evaluation.
Tests Administered
Rorschach
MMPI
Bender-Gestalt
Sentence Completion
Benjamin's Proverbs
Behavior During Examination
The patient was most deferent and conformed very readily to every requirement of the examination. He worked in a rapid and efficient manner, but made no spontaneous comments.
Analysis of Test Data
The impression from the psychological tests is that this is a man of considerably above average intelligence. He appears quite bright and alert and able to grasp most things rather quickly; however, he is intellectually lazy, putting little effort into dealing with the tasks before him. He tries to adhere to conventional lines of thinking predominantly, rather than reveal his own personal or idiosyncratic ideas.

This man's ability to exercise rational control tends to break down very quickly under conditions of affective stress. When these occasions intrude, the patient becomes completely unable to exercise reason and acts out in an impulsive, expansive manner. His concept of masculinity is rather superficial and he is completely unable to think of himself as a soft and gentle person. He is extremely narcissistic, feeling that any relationship to other people will act to his detriment. (For example, in interpreting the proverb "He travels swiftest who travels alone," the patient states, "Means what it says—no marriage or outside ties are good; just do things alone.")

The patient demonstrates considerable hostility towards women throughout. He tends to blame other people for his own failures and feels imposed upon by his associates. He resents authority, but finds it difficult to express these feelings directly.

Summary and Impressions

This patient seems to be a defensive and guarded individual suffering from much hostility and bitterness toward the world about him. Although he shows a slight tendency toward paranoid distortion, it is not sufficiently pronounced to be diagnostically valuable. When under affective stress his rational control becomes quite weak and he is prone to impulsive acting out. He demonstrates very little subjectively-felt anxiety and shows no characteristic neurotic symptomatology. The results of the psychological tests are most congruent with a diagnosis of sociopathic personality, with alcohol addiction as the major symptom.

13.

The following is a report of a patient thought to be suffering from an involutional condition. It includes the statement "She seems to have always had a considerable conflict about sex, on the one hand having an interest in such relationships, and on the other hand feeling that morally they should only serve the purpose of propagation." This formulation again illustrates the presence of complex concepts, such as ambivalence, expressed in a way comprehensible to a physician without special psychiatric training. The test data seem to reveal the dynamics associated with an involutional condition, thereby furnishing a supplementary, yet independent source from which the diagnosis can be derived.

Referred By

Physician for aid in diagnostic evaluation.

Test Administered

Rorschach	Sentence Completion
Bender-Gestalt	MMPI
Benjamin's Proverbs	

Behavior During Examination

This patient was cooperative during the examination, but extremely slow and apparently somewhat guarded during the process. It took her considerable time to complete the various tests. She sometimes tired during this process, especially in the early part of the testing session.

Analysis of Test Data

This woman's thinking has become very slow so that occasionally she is quite confused. She shows particular difficulty in generalizing or conceptualizing. Sometimes she tends to perseverate, substituting the solution of one problem for that of another where it is quite inappropriate. Her perceptions of situations and objects are sometimes only vaguely similar to their objective characteristics.

The patient is emotionally quite overcontrolled, tending to withdraw from stress through somatic symptom-formation. She has many vague fears and anxieties and her mood at present appears depressed. She feels inadequate, fearing that she will accomplish little in life and that whatever potential she had is diminishing with increasing age. She seems to have always had a considerable conflict about sex, on the one hand having an interest in such relationships, but on the other hand feeling that morally they should only serve the purpose of propagation. The fact that the latter is no longer possible has only exacerbated her conflict.

Her attitude toward others is one of caution. She is very sensitive to being rejected, but tries to deny this feeling. She seems to experience some bitterness towards the family and to blame her unfortunate environment for some of her present difficulties. There is also a tendency for her to exaggerate these difficulties and to be always suspicious of people and situations.

Summary and Impressions

The picture is that of a person who has slowed down considerably and whose thinking varies from being vague to being quite idiosyncratic. Although her reality ties in coping with practical situations appear relatively intact, her thought processes are characteristically confused and occasionally bizarre. Her mood is predominantly depressed, and she frequently reacts to stress through somatic symptom-formation. Psychological test results are most congruent with a diagnosis of involutional psychosis.

14.

In this report, the referring agent being a psychiatrist, the language and the concepts are at a higher level of complexity.

Note the distinction between those feelings attributed to the subjective frame of reference of the patient and those thought to be underlying motivational factors. An intermediate level consists of interests which are empirically compared with that of one or the other sex and may have various level references, depending on their context. The intent of the psychologist here is to serve as a consultant to assist in determining whether or not hospitalization is indicated.

Referred By
Psychiatrist for psychodiagnostic evaluation.

Tests Administered
Rorschach
TAT
MMPI (Incomplete)
Sentence Completion

Behavior During Examination
The patient was cooperative during the examination, but only with difficulty could she be prevailed upon to attend to the task and to refrain from ruminations about her condition and her past experiences. Interlarded throughout her test performance were many personal references, some of which were not too relevant.

Analysis of Test Data
This patient's thinking is quite confused and suffers from frequent interference by emergent unconscious material. She does not easily accept conventional lines of thought and is apparently experiencing great difficulty in dealing with the practical problems of everyday life. Rational control tends to disappear whenever affective stimulation becomes the least intense. Aggression seems a particular problem, being alternately directed towards the self in the form of depression, and towards others in the form of ideas of reference.

The patient subjectively feels very abused and hurt by other people. She feels especially hostile toward men and is generally quite blocked and concerned in the sexual area. She manifests certain masculine interests, while denying some of the feminine components of her personality. Her attitude toward her mother is fraught with ambivalence, while that toward her father is more strongly and consistently negative. She apparently feels that her own needs were frustrated early in childhood and that her early experiences have been detrimental to her.

The patient apparently is not using somatization as a defense because she denies any physical malaise. She uses fantasy as a major defense mechanism and sometimes shows elements of premorbidly compulsive activities and excessive ruminations. These ruminations are currently taking the form of paranoid delusions, some bodily in nature and some persecutory in content. The patient is also bothered by vague feelings of guilt, accompanied by depressive symptoms. Besides confessing to unusual religious experiences which she cannot specify, she admits to a history of acting out. At present acting out is still contemplated as an alternate technique for dealing with anxiety.

Summary and Impressions

The test data point to an acute schizophrenic condition character-ized by the emergence of much unconscious material, symbolic think-ing, ideas of reference, sexual panic, and mood swings. Consequently the impression is that this patient's condition is sufficiently serious to warrant hospitalization and that treatment can be more effectively undertaken in an inpatient setting.

15.

The psychological report here has a different flavor from any previously cited since it deals with a manifestly schizophrenic person. In spite of the blatant pathology revealed in the test data, an attempt is made to describe the unique way in which this particular patient reacts to the psychotic process. While his residual strengths are still described as of ultimate prog-nostic significance, at the same time the vagueness and tangen-tiality of his intellectual processes are clearly evident.

Referral

Physician for diagnostic evaluation.

Tests Administered

Rorschach

Bender-Gestalt

Wechsler-Bellevue, Form I

Behavior During Examination

This patient was courteous and compliant during the examination insofar as his condition permitted. He was extremely slow in all verbal situations, hesitating a long time before giving an answer and seeming to be very preoccupied. He required 45 minutes to draw the Bender figures and about three hours to complete the Wechsler-Belle-vue. He seemed very concerned as to whether he was doing a good job and requested constant reassurance from the examiner. A total of four sessions was needed to complete the examination.

Analysis of Data

Intellectually this patient is extremely sluggish and employs painful precision in his work without achieving any spectacular results. (His Full Scale IQ on the Wechsler-Bellevue was 110.) Generally, he succeeded better on those tasks such as tests of general information and vocabulary in which he could employ his past education and experience, but he performed poorly in those tests requiring social judgment or the ability to recognize and deal effectively with social situations. He seems completely unable to plan ahead, abstract matters being incomprehensible to him. His thinking is very stereotyped and perseverative in nature, and he seems obsessed by certain ideas of his own which interfere with his attention to reality. His intellectual ties to reality are quite inadequate. The test contained some indications that the patient may at one time have been more capable than appears at present. Generally, the more structured a situation, the better he can do.

The patient is very insecure and unsure of himself, requesting constant reassurance. He has no confidence in his perceptions of reality, feeling that he may be "clear off," as he once commented during the examination. His ability to distinguish between neutral and emotionally-loaded situations is quite impaired. He seems to recognize when emotion is appropriate, but is unable to meet the needs of other people or to give of himself in any interpersonal situation, being too preoccupied with his own problems. His concept of himself is that of a helpless individual who has inadequate controls over the situation, even though his level of aspiration in fantasy may be quite different. His affect appears quite flat and he does not show any particular tendencies toward acting out or being overtly unstable.

It is of diagnostic significance that this patient's thinking seems to be like a series of free associations. (For example, to one of the Rorschach cards he gave three different responses—a wildcat, a bobcat, and a tomcat—all to the same area.) In general, the tests indicated a good deal of perseverative thinking. When the patient gives a correct answer, it is usually contaminated in some way by schizoid elements. (For example, in answering what he would do with an envelope that he found in the street, he replied that he would mail it, but adding that if it were suspicious he would turn it over to the police. Asked to define the word "belfry," he explained that it is "the top of something like the top of a church where the bells are kept," later adding that "it is the top of a human being, like when people say 'He's got bats in his belfry.' ") The impression deriving from the psychological tests is that of a sluggish, apathetic person who shows considerable disturbance in his thought processes. The test patterns support the diagnosis of schizophrenia with catatonic elements predominating, as well as occasional tendencies toward paranoid thinking.

16.

This illustration is that of a re-evaluation. The patient had been previously examined by means of psychological tests and subsequently had been treated by a psychiatrist who requested a re-evaluation in order to determine the progress made and her condition of the moment. A perusal of the report suggests that psychological test data, from the perspective of the patient, has certainly improved in some areas, but not without some apparent loss in others. The over-all effect is evaluated, but in a discriminating fashion. A concluding attempt is made to summarize the therapeutic benefits and to suggest to the therapist new directions in which to move. This is an example of a specific request which has been met appropriately. Such longitudinal use of psychological data is of special interest and deserves much further exploration.

Referred By

Psychiatrist for re-evaluation to determine possible acting out and the advisability of hospitalization rather than continuation on an outpatient basis.

Tests Administered

Rorschach

TAT

Behavior During Examination

This patient readily conformed to the examination requirements and showed no overt reluctance to do any of the things asked. Her reactions were exceedingly slow and were interspersed by long pauses. For example, she would take a TAT card, regard it for four or five minutes, then the story would come out in a rush of words. This behavior leads the examiner to believe that this woman tends to think about a problem rather carefully and to work out a solution in her mind before ever verbalizing it.

Analysis of Test Data

Present indications are that this is an inhibited, exceedingly sloweddown individual who believes in keeping her feelings to herself and

who seems to be extremely preoccupied, her thinking being characterized by rumination and daydreams. Currently she appears to have good
ties to reality and possesses ability to think along conventional lines,
but she is still somewhat depressed.

In comparing her present test performance with that obtained
earlier, a number of changes are evident: The most favorable changes
are that (1) this patient has considerably better control over her
emotions, is less impulsive and less of an actor-out than she was
a year ago, and (2) her perceptions are more realistic and her thinking
is more flexible and less affected by overt bizarre ideation. These im-
provements have taken place at the expense of some spontaneity in
the expression of feelings that was formerly present to some extent.
She is more inclined to try to avoid unpleasantness and to escape into
fantasy when reality seems to be frustrating her needs. She shows less
aggression, but still displays some passive opposition of the kind that
has characterized her in the past.

Summary and Clinical Impressions

This patient is able to present a surface appearance of rationality
and conventionality almost all of the time, though at the cost of considerable inhibition and repression of her needs. She tends to escape
into fantasy under the pressure of her present reality situation. The
impression is that of a primarily affective disorder of the depressive
type characterized by feelings of withdrawal, loneliness, and frustration, which are not expressed overtly. There seems little danger that
this patient will act out either bizarre, impulsive behavior, or suicide
at the present time since she is quite controlled. The effects of psychotherapy are primarily manifested in this increasingly-effective and
more flexible control over both her behavior and thinking and in the
almost complete disappearance of bizarre ideation. Considerable depression and escape through fantasy still remains evident.

17.

The final illustration consists of the psychological evaluation
of a marriage. The focus here is not solely on the personality
assets and liabilities of the marital partners, but on their relationship as such. The writing of such a report is preceded by a
parallel analysis of all of the psychological tests with each
stimulus being considered in terms of the responses elicited from
each partner and what this may imply for their joint reaction
and interaction in a given life situation. Please note the section

on "analysis of the marriage" which is the unique feature of this kind of report.*

Referred By
Attorney for marital evaluation and possible counseling.

Tests Administered
Bender-Gestalt
WAIS
Rorschach
MMPI
SCT

Behavioral Observation and Analysis of Test Data
Mrs. Jones. Mrs. Jones is a small, dark woman who is thin to the point of emaciation. She seemed quite comfortable during the examination and talked freely and at great length. She gave the initial impression of a woman of above average intelligence and social skills.

Despite the examiner's impression, test results indicated that Mrs. Jones functions fairly consistently at the dull normal level of intelligence, though there is reason to believe that at some earlier time in her life she performed more efficiently than she does at present. This woman's ties to reality are very tenuous. Under very little provoaction her facade breaks down and she retreats to fantasy and is likely at such times to behave in an irrational manner.

Mrs. Jones is highly sensitive to others but only as they meet or fail to meet her needs. She feels misunderstood and appears convinced that the solution to her life problems lies in the hands of outside agents. Despite her sensitivity, which is of the grandiose variety, Mrs. Jones is singularly lacking in empathy. While she attempts to portray the role of loving wife and mother, she is actually so tied up in her own infantile needs that she cannot actually function in an adult, responsible fashion.

The major conflict in Mrs. Jones' life appears to be centered in the area of needs for nurturence versus adult responsibility. The infantile needs appear to have taken precedence. She attempts to handle her problems mainly by perseveration and fantasy. These techniques are used so extensively as to suggest a psychotic adjustment with its attendent bizarre behavior.

Mr. Jones. Mr. Jones is a nice-appearing, friendly man with a some-

* This report was prepared in collaboration with Charlotte David and Carol Bowdish.

what effeminate appearance. He seemed relaxed during the examination and talked readily and easily about his problems.

On semistructured tasks where it could quickly be determined what the test was "getting at" Mr. Jones became evasive and cautious in his answers. As the tasks became increasingly ambiguous, he found it necessary to approach things as a whole and to impose his own structure upon the items.

Mr. Jones' intellectual efficiency is within the very superior range. He is able to use his ability in a consistent and effective manner at the present time. His basic conflicts are centered around independence versus dependence, passivity versus aggressiveness, feelings of inadequacy and difficulty in sexual identification. Those conflicts are handled by use of the following mechanisms: intellectualization, distanciation, evasion, and rationalization. The client is a sensitive and creative man whose needs are not being met. His feelings of inadequacy often cause him to fear close relationships with others and to resort to an increasingly impersonal, superficial, defensive and manipulative manner as a means of protection.

He requires support and reassurance from others and has a desire to be loved, cared for and to play the submissive role. He may at times handle problems by leaving and finding satisfaction with others. However, Mr. Jones shows flexible, rational control and it is the examiner's feeling that he can adequately cope with the ordinary stresses of life.

Analysis of the Marriage

The difficulties between Mr. and Mrs. Jones appear to arise out of a basic inability to meet on common ground. Intellectually Mr. Jones is far superior to his wife but, since her reactions to stress are highly irrational, he is not able to understand or cope with her behavior. Perhaps one reason he is having difficulty is because he has been taken in by her ability to appear eccentric rather than irrational and dull.

Socially and emotionally, Mrs. Jones plays the role of the superfeminine woman who needs to be taken care of, understood, and loved. Her needs in this area are insatiable. Mr. Jones is somewhat feminine in his needs and interest and is most comfortable playing the passive role. Consequently, they cannot begin to satisfy each other. Initially Mr. Jones may have been attracted by his wife's apparently excessive femininity because it made him feel more adequate. Mrs. Jones in turn may have seen Mr. Jones as a strong, understanding, sensitive man.

Summary and Recommendations

Both the members of this marriage seem to possess the same type of characterological structure, but on different levels. His pattern is a neurotic one, while hers is psychotic. He has a considerable amount of flexible, rational control at his command but Mrs. Jones is very rigid. Prognostically there seems little hope that much can be done to help Mrs. Jones. Her difficulties appear to be of long standing and relatively intractable. Since it is our feeling that no one could possibly be the kind of person Mrs. Jones wishes her husband to be, we might perhaps be of most assistance by helping Mr. Jones to gain a truer understanding of his wife's condition.

REFERENCES

1. Behn, S. Ueber die Kunst des Praktisch brauehbaren Gutachtens. *Psychologische Beitraege*, 1957, *1*, 362–385.
2. Bellak, L. *The TAT and CAT in Clinical Use*. New York: Grune & Stratton, 1954.
3. Datel, W. E., & Gengerelli, J. A. The reliability of Rorschach interpretations. *J. proj. Tech.*, 1955, *19*, 372–380.
4. Davenport, Beverly F. The semantic validity of TAT interpretations. *J. consult. Psychol.*, 1952, *16*, 171–175.
5. Deri, Susan K. *Introduction to the Szondi Test*. New York: Grune & Stratton, 1949.
6. English, H. B., & English, A. C. *A Comprehensive Dictionary of Psychological and Psychoanalytical Terms*. New York: Longmans, Green & Co., 1958.
7. Forer, B. R. The fallacy of personal validation: A classroom demonstration of gullibility. *J. abnorm. soc. Psychol.*, 1949, *44*, 118–123.
8. Forer, B. R. A structured sentence completion test. *J. proj. Tech.*, 1950, *14*, 15–30.
9. Foster, A. Writing psychological reports. *J. clin. Psychol.*, 1951, 7, 195.
10. Garfield, S. L., Heine, R. W., & Leventhal, M. An evaluation of psychological reports in a clinical setting. *J. consult. Psychol.*, 1954, *18*, 281–286.
11. Grayson, H. M., & Tolman, R. S. A semantic study of concepts of clinical psychologists and psychiatrists. *J. abnorm. soc. Psychol.*, 1950, *45*, 216–231.
12. Hammond, K. R., & Allen, J. M. *Writing Clinical Reports*. New York: Prentice-Hall, Inc., 1953.
13. Holzberg, J. D., Alessi, S. L., & Wexler, M. Psychological case reporting at psychiatric staff conferences. *J. consult. Psychol.*, 1951, *15*, 425–429.
14. Hooker, Evelyn. Male homosexuality in the Rorschach. *J. proj. Tech.*, 1958, 22, 36–55.
15. Klopfer, W. G., & Borstelmann, L. J. The associative valences of the Szondi pictures. *J. Pers.*, 1950, *19*, 172–188.
16. Leary, T. *The Interpersonal Diagnosis of Personality*. New York: Ronald Press Co., 1957.
17. Lodge, G. T. How to write a psychological report. *J. clin. Psychol.*,

1953, *9*, 400–402.
18. Palmer, J. O. The organization of the clinical psychological study. Unpublished manuscript.
19. Robinson, J. T., & Cohen, L. D. Individual bias in psychological reports. *J. clin. Psychol.*, 1954, *10*, 333–336.
20. Sargent, Helen. *The Insight Test.* New York: Grune & Stratton, 1953.
21. Shneidman, E. S. Make a picture story test. *Genet. Psychol. Mono.*, 1948, *38*, 145–223.
22. Suczek, R. F., & Klopfer, W. G. Interpretation of the Bender-Gestalt test: The associative value of the figures. *J. orthopsychiat.*, 1952, 22, 62–75.
23. Sundberg, N. D. The acceptability of "fake" versus "bona fide" personality test interpretation. *J. abnorm. soc. Psychol.*, 1955, *50*, 145–147.
24. Tallent, N. On individualizing the psychologists' clinical evaluation. *J. clin. Psychol.*, 1958, *14*, 243–245.
25. Teicher, A. A clinical appraoch to reporting. In R. Watson (Ed.) *Readings in the Clinical Method in Psychology.* New York: Harper & Bros., 1949, p. 244.
26. The O.S.S. Assessment Staff. *Assessment of Men.* New York: Rinehart & Co., Inc. 1948.
27. Ullman, L. P., Berkman, V. C., & Hamister, R. C. Psychological reports related to behavior and benefit of placement in home care. *J. clin. Psychol.*, 1958, *14*, 254–259.

GENERAL INDEX

Administrative decisions, 11
Alessi, S. L., 2, 24, 27, 33, 53-54
Allen, J. M., 1, 4, 10, 13, 18-19, 23-24, 26, 29, 32, 52

Behavior
during examination, 37-40, 75, 108
prediction of, 1, 7, 11-12
Behn, S., 20-21
Bellak, L., 30-31
Bender Visual-Motor Gestalt Test 39, 41, 44, 45, 51, 102-105, 108, 110
Benjamin's Proverbs, 78-79, 108, 109, 111, 113
Berkman, V. C., 7, 12
Blacky Pictures, 69, 84-88, 110, 111, 112, 113
"Blind" interpretation, 62
Borstelman, L. J., 58, 105
Bowdish, Carol, 140n

Children's Apperception Test, 48
Client
expectation of, 5-6
responsibility for, 5, 62-63
Cohen, L. D., 71, 72
Competence of Psychologist
level of, 20, 28

Datel, W. E., 15-16
Davenport, Beverly F., 15
David, Charlotte, 140n
Deri, Susan K., 70
Diagnosis
evaluation of, 48-49
specification of, 8-9

Diagnostic signs
use of, 8
Draw-A-Person Test, 15-16, 39, 56, 70, 105-108, 109, 111, 112

Ego-Psychology, 30-31, 45, 63
English, A. C., 57
English, H. B., 57
Ethical problems, 29

Forer, B. R., 14, 18, 80n
Foster, A., 13, 18, 24, 53
Freud, S., 69, 70

Garfield, S. L., 7, 71-72
Gengerelli, J. A., 15-16
Grayson, H. M., 54-55, 56-57

Hamister, R. C., 7, 12
Hammond, K. R., 1, 4, 10, 13, 18-19, 23-24, 26, 29, 32, 52
Heine, R. W., 7, 71
Holzberg, J. D., 2, 24, 27, 33, 53-54
Hooker, Evelyn, 9

Illustrative reports
ego-psychological, 31-32
Personality-area oriented, 115-142
of adults, 119-142
of children, 115-119
psychoanalytic, 21-22
problem-oriented, 27-28
re-evaluation, 138-139
test-oriented, 25-26
Intelligence, 40-41